STA-... Industries
Health Dept.

Goodbye Backache

Goodbye Backache

The practical way to a pain-free and healthy back.
Eighty million North Americans suffer back pain.
Don't be one of them.

Dr. David Imrie
with Colleen Dimson

A PRENTICE-HALL/NEWCASTLE BOOK

Copyright © 1983 David Imrie

Newcastle Publishing Limited
30 Howland Avenue
Toronto, Ontario, M5R 3B3, Canada

Published in Canada by:

Prentice-Hall Canada Inc.
1870 Birchmount Road
Scarborough, Ontario, M1P 2J7, Canada

and simultaneously in the United States by Arco Publishing, Inc.

Canadian Cataloguing in Publication Data
Imrie, David.

Goodbye backache

Includes index.
ISBN 0-13-360263-X

1. Backache.   I. Dimson, Colleen.   II. Title.

RD768.I57   617′.56′052   C82-094348-7

Printed and bound in Canada.

Contents

To Dr. Wilf Auger
who was profound in his simplicity.

1

Backache: The 20th Century Affliction

Every day in my office I listen to patients tell me about their backaches. "What do you think caused it?" I ask them. Do any of their replies sound familiar to you?

"It's natural; I'm getting older."

"I've been working too hard and something had to give—it was my back."

"I've got a slipped disc."

"I lifted something the wrong way and it injured my back."

"Weak backs run in my family."

"My back aches because my bed is too soft."

Not one of my patients has ever said to me: "My back is aching because my back muscles are weak and I have poor posture." Nor do I expect them to offer this explanation. Very few people have ever been properly educated as to how the back functions nor has it been explained to them why strong muscles and good posture will help prevent backache.

The purpose of this book then, is fourfold: (1) to demonstrate how poor posture and weak muscles contribute to common low backache; (2) to offer a test by which you can determine the fitness of your back; (3) to show you the simple exercises that will help prevent backache for the rest of your life; (4) to show you how to use your back more effectively in your day-to-day activities.

There was a time when I was as confused as my patients about the cause of low back pain. Fortunately, I had the chance to study it in thousands of patients and because of this opportunity my perceptions of backache began to change. I'd like to tell you how it all came about and why I now run the Back Care Centre in Toronto.

As a doctor I consider myself to be in a very unusual position: I see patients when they are healthy as well as when they are sick. Now, wait a minute, you're probably thinking, don't all doctors? No, not really. Think back to the last time you went to a doctor. Aside from going for the occasional check-up, you were most likely there because you weren't feeling well. The family practitioner usually sees patients when there is something wrong with them. And that goes for the specialist as well. When was the last time you saw a specialist? Were you there because you felt terrific or because you had a health problem? The odds are that you were not feeling well and had been sent to the specialist by your family doctor.

Because I wear two hats—I'm a family practitioner and an industrial physician—my experience is unique. Every year I give several thousand medicals in my industrial practice and the majority of these people have few complaints. These examinations determine employees' fitness for work and their ability to withstand future illness or injury. These are health-oriented rather than disease-oriented examinations. The rest of the time in my family practice I see patients who are sick and in pain and, because it has become so common in our society, they are often complaining about backache. I can assure you that in my family practice I have never had a patient ask me to examine his or her back unless it was causing trouble. Otherwise they take it for granted that their backs are in good shape. They could be wrong. In fact, they often are. When you consider the prevalence of back problems in North America, there is a good likelihood that the day will soon come when they end up in my office asking me to treat their aching backs.

As a young doctor leaving medical school I had the good fortune to become associated with Dr. Wilf Auger, who had started an industrial medical practice in the 1940s. However, at the time I didn't know how important his approach to practising medicine would be to me later. The truth was that I hated the work. I thought industrial medicine was a drag, that it had no real meaning, and I decided that as soon as my family practice was flourishing, I'd get out of industrial medicine as fast as I could.

In the meantime, while working with Dr. Auger, I began to realize that he was a fascinating man who was showing me a side of medicine my university training had not provided. Dr. Auger believed that a doctor should always try to take a simple approach to healing whenever possible. "David," he'd say, "sometimes you forget some of the basics when you are treating patients. Take that man who just left the office with the badly cut finger. You stitched it up, but until I advised you, you weren't going to put a splint on it so the finger would rest. I guess you didn't realize that without the splint he'd be using his finger more than he should and it would take much longer to heal."

Dr. Auger's simple approach sometimes had profound results. For example, although I'd been using it for years I hadn't realized that the Auger Suction, a simple plastic tube used around the world to get a culture from children's throats, had been developed by him. So because of Dr. Auger's influence at a crucial point in my life, I began thinking for myself and taking a more broadly based approach to some medical problems. Now there's no question that certain illnesses call for standard treatment: appendicitis requires an operation, fractured limbs must be immobilized, questionable lumps or growths must be excised. However, many other problems—such as headaches and backaches—are far from clearcut and often do not lend themselves to the standard medical approach.

My change in attitude helped me to see that there was tremendous potential in the field of industrial medicine. I had come into the field in 1969. In those days, many companies fired problem workers. An alcoholic who wasn't doing the job was simply pushed out the door. But employees were slowly gaining more job security because of union agreements and government legislation, and companies couldn't fire them as easily as in the past. This put the companies in a bind. It was harder to fire the employees, and yet they couldn't afford poor job performance. Since then, the trend has been toward the development of employee assistance programs to help workers with drinking problems or with any personal troubles that prevent them from working effectively.

While alcoholism and social and mental health problems cost industry a lot of money because of time lost on the job, back pain remains the biggest problem of all. It costs billions of dollars a year in North America. In Ontario, the province in Canada where I work, 125 million dollars a year is spent solely on medical and compensation payments for employees who are off work because of back problems.

In my practice, I began to see the terrible waste of human potential. If industry was concerned about the waste of dollars, I was just as concerned about the waste of people. Decent and hard-working, they didn't want to cause any trouble and yet, because of back problems, they were unable to effectively perform their jobs. Often desperate after years of recurring back pain, they would pin their hopes on an operation that they thought would finally cure them, only to be told that their problem wasn't severe enough for that kind of radical treatment. At this point the company would often decide that job reassignment was the solution.

Let's take the case of Joe S., a forty-year-old tool-and-die maker who had developed a bad back. The company he worked for finally put him in the storage room performing light duties. Joe was really scared now and beginning to feel useless. Here he was, a skilled worker, doing the kind of work reserved for the older guys with bad health. Joe began to avoid doing everything that makes life worth living. He stopped playing sports with his friends; he was afraid to roughhouse with his kids; he left it to his wife to cut the grass and take out the garbage. Even his sex life deteriorated because of Joe's worry about his back. And bad as all this was, Joe knew it could get worse. Suppose the company did a productivity survey? Joe could be pensioned off early or let go because his job was considered redundant.

In my work as an industrial doctor, I saw what happened to Joe happen to other workers, time and time again. I was terribly frustrated—I had so little to offer workers who suffered from backache except rest and pain relief. I *had* to find a better way. It took me several years and I did come up with a new approach, but only because I changed my perception of the working back. The main purpose of this book is to change the way you think about your back. With this in mind, take a look at the following case histories. I think they will intrigue anyone who has ever suffered from backache.

Wooden Chopsticks
(The story of Mike N.)

On March 8, 1941, while fighting with the British army in Java, I was taken prisoner by the Japanese and transported to Boei Glodok penitentiary in Batavia, now called Jakarta. The conditions in the prison were deplorable. We slept on concrete floors in cells overrun with roaches up to three inches long. We were given only three cups of soggy rice a day and this had to sustain us while we worked on our first project, the airport runways.

At the prison the men were dying left, right, and centre because of malnutrition and tropical diseases for which there was no medication. I volunteered to join a work force required for Japan in the hope that I might have a better chance of survival if I could get away from the dysentery and tropical fevers that were killing my fellow prisoners.

The voyage from Java aboard the *Dia Nichi Maru* was a nightmare. We were housed in the bilges of the ship with only enough room to lie down or stand. Once a day we were allowed up on deck for an hour. Dysentery and disease were rampant and every day men died and were buried at sea. Our first port of call was Singapore, where they transferred us to another ship where the conditions were just as inhuman. After surviving a typhoon at sea, when we thought for sure we were going to capsize, we finally disembarked at Hakodate in northern Japan.

Dressed only in khaki shorts and suffering terribly from the cold we were marched to a prison camp called Biaba. The buildings were wooden sheds where we were each allocated one sleep area, which consisted of a straw mat, six feet by three feet in size. The food was terrible. Our basic diet consisted of three cups of white rice a day with fish-head soup or, as a special delicacy, horseradish soup.

The work force was split into two groups called the "dock force" and the "kryac force." The dock force worked in the shipyard doing menial physical tasks. The kryac force, to which I was assigned, loaded and unloaded ships and barges in the harbour. We carried bulk cement and bulk salt weighing about 130 pounds per bag and we worked ten hours a day, stopping only for lunch (if you could call it that), seven days a week with one Sunday a month off to clean the camp.

Every man in the camp carried the sign of one disease or another. Septicemia was prevalent and everyone had beriberi from lack of vitamins. Beriberi attacked in two ways: the type I had was called "dry" and affected the nervous system. It produced terrible pain in the feet and legs, which would convulse periodically. Any kind of movement was agony. The other type was painless but more serious. The body filled with fluids to such an extent that it eventually drowned the prisoner. Septicemia was another disease I had. It attacked in different ways—some of the men had huge boils all over their bodies, while in others their hands swelled to three times the normal size and filled up with pus. I had septic blisters from my fingertips to the top of my arms.

After two years as a prisoner my weight was down to 110 pounds and I was now unloading boxes of fish weighing about 150 pounds. Two Japanese would lift up the box, drop it on your shoulders and away you went from barge to freezer, a distance of about 50 yards. After three years, my weight was down to 100 pounds. The work now consisted of loading coal barges in the bay. A team of ten men would unload the coal from the railway cars, shovel it into baskets on a bamboo pole, and carry it to the boat where they unloaded it into the hold. To do this we had to manoeuvre across the water on a series of wooden planks—up one side and down another. When full, the baskets weighed about 200 pounds and if one man loaded as much as 10 to 12 tons of coal, this was considered a good day's work by the Japanese.

I was amazed at the strength and agility displayed by the Japanese work force at that time. All of them, whether they were 20 or 60 years of age, were in top physical condition. They were all very muscular no matter what their builds—heavy, medium, or slight—and there wasn't an ounce of surplus flesh on their bodies. I was also amazed at the prisoners' adaptability; we kept going until we were ready to drop.

During my three and a half years of incarceration my weight dropped from 165 pounds to 90 pounds, but I survived despite contracting dysentery, beriberi, bronchial pneumonia, mastoiditis, and septicemia. I also had eye problems, severe frostbite, and injuries from blows inflicted by rifle butts. The one thing I never did suffer during the whole of that period was a backache. Nor can I recall even one complaint about backache from the other prisoners during the years we were forced to do such heavy work.

The one observation I did make during my imprisonment was that the younger men—in their early twenties—seemed to be in better condition than the men who were a few years older. I also noticed that the fatter a prisoner was at the beginning of this misery, the worse off he was. I was physically strong and quite muscular when I was taken prisoner and I'm sure this gave me a considerable advantage. The mind also exerts a powerful force when it comes to survival.

A Silver Spoon
(The story of David B.)

The first time I ever had an attack of back pain I was lying on a beach at Marseilles. My parents had sent me on a trip to Europe as a reward for the high grades I had achieved in private school. I mean, I couldn't believe it had happened to me—it seemed ridiculous to have a back spasm at the age of 19. When I tried to get up I just doubled over with the pain and had to be half carried to the hotel where a French doctor gave me medication. I ended up lying flat on my back for three days in my hotel room, staring at the ceiling and reviewing my life.

As lives go, I guess I couldn't complain, even if the life of a rich man's son isn't always as wonderful as it looks to an outsider. Who wouldn't opt to be part of the best-fed, best-schooled, best-dressed crowd, if they had the chance? Living up to my father's expectations wasn't always easy, though. After I finished private school, where I'd played the mandatory cricket, squash, and tennis, he insisted I attend military college for a year. "It'll make a man of you," he told me. I put in my stint but I never took to the life there. For one thing, I hated the military posture they drilled into us. It felt ridiculous and unnatural and I also found that it was very fatiguing.

I was relieved when I entered university and enjoyed it tremendously. I'd decided on the law for a career and I never minded the long hours of study. I played sports to compensate for all the hours of grinding at the books and I thought I was in pretty good shape. You can imagine how mystified I was when I had a bad attack of back pain after driving to an out-of-town football game during my last year of university. However, like the first attack, it disappeared relatively quickly after a few days rest in bed.

Life proceeded fairly pleasantly. I obtained my law degree at the age of 27, joined an established firm, and met my wife, Kate, who is the light of my life along with our two children. I guess Kate was the first woman I ever dated who clued into the fact that I have a bit of an inferiority complex. She used to kid me about my slouching posture. I'm not the best-dressed man on the block either—in fact, I suppose you could say I'm a bit of a slob when it comes to clothes. I thought about it one day when Kate was riding me about my "slumpiness," as she dubbed it, and it dawned on me that my appearance was somehow tied up with my feelings about my father. He's a tall, aggressive, domineering man, the kind whose subordinates jump when he's around. I never liked the way he dictated to his employees. I knew I didn't want to handle people that way and I guess I didn't want to resemble him even physically.

It was during my early thirties that I began to worry a little about my back. I noticed that it was beginning to feel stiff in the mornings or after long car trips. A hard day in court brought on a lot of back twinges and discomfort and I attributed it to stress. Then I had a very bad attack which kept me away from work last year for nearly a month. I'd just turned 35. I was playing squash and out it went. It was sheer agony. The diagnosis was low back pain due to muscular strain. I have to admit that I was scared. I felt like an old man lying around all that time and it seemed to take forever before my back felt really good again.

That last attack left me feeling rather nervous about playing squash but I also feel that without exercise to relieve tension I'll be in even worse shape. I love practising law but I think I'll have to reduce my work load. I'm sure that it will help because I'm convinced that my back problems are caused by stress.

Why Does Your Back Ache?

I'm sure you have some questions about those two case histories. They are probably the same questions that began occurring to me in my industrial practice and that led to my new system of back care. Here we have two young men of approximately the same age—one living in terrible conditions, suffering from malnutrition, and at the same time required to do the work of a dray horse for three years, lifting loads unheard of in our North American factories. And yet he never once suffered from backache. The other young man is living under optimum conditions—in fact, he was on vacation when he had his first attack of back pain—and yet he suffers from a recurrent back problem that finally began to alter his life. Is the young lawyer's back pain really caused by stress as he so firmly believes? If so, why did he get his first attack while he was relaxing on vacation? It seems he has discounted the episodes in his youth. He shouldn't. They were the first warnings that he was in for more trouble later on. Attacks of low back pain are indicators that the back is not in good condition and needs strengthening. I'll explain more about such early warning signals later. To return to stress, there is no doubt that his work does have stressful elements, but surely the POWs were living under more stressful conditions than any of us will ever likely face. They spent every day in a struggle for physical and mental survival. Why didn't they get backaches? Could the lawyer's back pain be the result of a heavy work load? When we consider the average working day in the prison camp the question seems redundant.

Is it because the lawyer's bed is too soft or too hard? Is it because his car seat is not properly adjusted? He said his back was stiff in the mornings and after long car rides. Let's go back to the prison camp again. The men slept on straw mats on the floor for years while suffering from terrible diseases. None of them ever complained of back pain.

Could it be age, could it be heredity, or could it just be plain bad luck? Or could the precipitating cause be something so simple that few back sufferers, including the lawyer, ever take it into account? Could the lawyer's backache, and yours, be caused by *poor posture* and *weak muscles*?

The Right Questions

It wasn't until I, too, began asking the right questions in my medical practice that I was able to come up with an approach for preventing common backache. My first breakthrough came one day when I was examining a male patient who had returned to my office with his second attack of low back pain in just a few months. I had just finished a routine examination of a pregnant patient who was also complaining of backache and, as I was considering the man's back problem, it occurred to me that he looked just as pregnant as the lady who had just left my office. But the lady was eventually going to lose the weight on her abdomen and, with the right exercise for her stretched muscles, she would return to normal. The man wasn't going to lose his stomach, however, unless he took some drastic action. So I began putting my back patients with pot bellies on diets. It helped some but it didn't work for all of them, so I knew that although I was on the right track, it wasn't the complete solution.

At about this time, my sister, Janet, a physiotherapist who was working in Vancouver, returned for a summer vacation and we spent some time together at our family cottage. "Jan," I told her one evening, "I'm having real problems trying to help patients with low back pain. It's the worst problem in industry because it engenders so much frustration and suspicion." She was intrigued. It so happened that she had been working on a research project on treatments for back problems. We decided that she would return to Toronto and work with me in my office. We would see what the two of us could learn about back care for industrial workers.

During the next few years, we began to have considerable success with the exercises Jan prescribed in the office for workers complaining about low back pain. It was especially gratifying to see the change in the workers' attitudes. Once they understood how the exercises would strengthen the back muscles so that there was less wear and tear on the spine, they became conscientious about the simple routine they were asked to perform for only a few minutes each day. Instead of being off work every few months with recurring attacks of back pain, the workers were now able to go for much longer periods without back problems—years instead of months. Their whole outlook on life became positive once they knew that there was a method they could easily employ to remain free from back pain or to control it if there was a flare-up.

I then began to wonder if our exercise program could not be applied to people *before* they had a backache. Why wait until they had an attack and were in discomfort? Jan and I began to study 700 to 1,000 backs a year and from our research we began to learn how to tell whether a person's back was strong, normal, or weak. We developed what I call the National Back Fitness Test, a system of measurement that is presented in Chapter 6. This test will enable you to determine the shape your back is in and what you can do about it. If you are one of the millions of North Americans suffering from common backache, it is almost certain that you will eventually have a serious back disorder unless you take steps now to strengthen your back. The exercises we recommend are easy, painless, *and* effective. No matter what your back problem, this book shows you how to control back pain and lead a happier, healthier life.

2

Back Talk

"We see what we are trained to see," Michelangelo said. This is especially true when it comes to backache. Most professionals, quite naturally, deal with backache according to the perspective in which they have been trained. The safety professional sees backache as the end result of an unsafe condition—for example, because there was an oil slick on the factory floor, a worker slipped and hurt his back. The safety engineer or ergonomist approaches backache from the standpoint of looking at the unusual stresses placed upon the body by the improper design of equipment in the workplace. The family doctor sees backache as a pain problem—relieve the pain, remedy the problem. The orthopedic surgeon focuses on bones and discs, the osteopath and chiropractor on a misaligned bone or subluxed joint that can be manipulated into place, the psychiatrist on hysterical or conversion reactions in backache.

Most people probably never give their backs a second thought until they begin to hurt. Unlike new cars, people don't come into the world with repair manuals attached and most have never been educated as to how the back works and why it responds in certain ways. That is why patients become more and more uneasy as they discover that the diagnosis of backache is one of exclusion—more geared to what it *isn't* than to what it is. Faced with so many different professional explanations for the backache, the patient's uneasiness often turns into anxiety as he or she begins to think that nobody knows for sure what is wrong.

The following sections clear up some of the prevalent misconceptions people have about their backs. How well do *you* know your own back?

Around the World
and Back

True or false?: At some period in their lives, three out of four people will suffer from backache.

That statistic is often used to emphasize the magnitude of the problem in western society, and there is no doubt that the oft-quoted North American statistics are staggering in their implications:

On any given day in North America 6.8 million people are confined to bed with backache. New cases occur at the rate of 1.5 million a month.
More than 200,000 North Americans a year undergo back surgery.
Every year in North America, there are 200 million workdays lost due to back problems.
North Americans spend 6 billion dollars a year for tests and treatment by a dizzying array of back specialists, including orthopedists, osteopaths, physiotherapists, chiropractors, and self-styled healers.
Of the 75 million backache victims in the United States, 5 million are partly disabled and 2 million are unable to work at all. It's estimated that four out of five Americans will eventually be forced off their feet by pain in their backs.
Time lost from work for the treatment of back pain costs North American industry an estimated 15 billion dollars annually.

Disheartening statistics aren't they? Do they include you and your back? Don't worry—by the time you've finished this book, you'll have been shown a way to avoid and control backache and you'll be able to thumb your nose at those figures for the rest of your life.

By now you most likely believe the answer to the leading statement is true; that indeed, three out of four people will suffer from backache at some point in their lives. But the statement is misleading—it is not true because it does not take into account people in other parts of the world. Do they suffer from backache as much as North Americans?

A few years ago, while studying the spread of heart disease in different countries and cultures, I became curious about whether the incidence of back disease was as high in developing countries as it was in North America. I began to question surgeons returning from Africa, India, and Malaysia. They were surprised by the question because they had rarely seen a patient who complained of backache. Operations on the back were almost unknown in those countries. When I questioned immigrant patients from the same countries they reinforced the doctors' statements. They, too, testified to the scarcity of back complaints in their homelands.

By now, tremendously intrigued, I wrote letters to the authorities at the International Labour Office in Geneva, a world body that studies working conditions and health problems in workers around the world. I asked for any data they had on the incidence of diseases of the vertebrae among workers in developing countries.

A letter from Dr. A. David, medical officer for the Office of Occupational Health, confirmed that they had no such data. He wrote, "It has not been distinguished if back pain is really rare due to different work loads and work postures (less mechanized work) or if the problem was overwhelmed by more serious health problems like parasitic or infectious diseases and malnutrition." He added that, in his opinion, "the former probability seemed to be more plausible." Further searching on my part corroborated Dr. David's statement about the lack of data.

Finally, however, I did discover a paper, "Lumbar Intervertebral Disc Disease in Africans," by Laurence F. Levy of University College Medical School in Salisbury, Rhodesia (now, of course, Zimbabwe). Dr. Levy wrote that although "it was certainly true that only a minority of African people who were sick attended hospital, back and leg pain can be very crippling so that it is reasonable to suppose that a fair percentage of those afflicted will seek medical care." And yet the incidence of back problems in Rhodesia was considerably higher among Europeans than among Africans. According to Dr. Levy, it appeared that "the syndrome of herniation of the intervertebral disc as it is known in its classical form rarely occurs in Africans." Dr. Levy found it surprising "that the incidence is so low since heavy manual labour is so universal among African people." He summarized his report by stating "that there are no obvious gross anatomical differences in the spines of the two races and that the incidence of degenerative conditions of the spine is the same. We have found, however, that the mobility of the spines of Africans is considerably greater than that of Europeans. We suggest that the greater mobility of the spines as well as the widespread prevalence of manual labour as an occupation may be factors contributing to the low incidence of herniated intervertebral discs not only among Africans but among native populations in other underdeveloped parts of the world." Dr. Levy also conjectured that manual labour strengthens rather than weakens the muscles and ligaments supporting the back and, therefore, reduces the likelihood of disc herniation.

So you see, back pain does not affect three out of four people in the world. Only in the western world where society is highly automated is backache so prevalent. Backache can be characterized as a hypokinetic disease, which means that inactivity and a sedentary style of life are major factors contributing to it. In an increasingly automated world where most work, travel, and play are done sitting down, backs become ever more vulnerable to injury.

Looking Back

True or false?: With increasing automation in the workplace, back trouble is becoming less of a problem.

We are all aware that 20th-century technology has reduced man's labour to the point where it is estimated that in North America 75 per cent of the labour force do their jobs sitting down. Not only do we sit down on the job, we sit watching TV at night, we sit in our cars driving to work or on business trips, we sit in aeroplanes flying off to vacations where, out of shape and exhausted from so much sitting, we lie down on a beach to relax.

Because our bodies are human machines designed to adapt to constant activity, the sedentary lives we lead are creating new physical problems. Unless selected activity replaces the physical activity we once maintained through work, we cannot stay vigorous and healthy. Hans Selye, the Canadian expert on stress, has written, "Adaptation is the criterion of the living organism." Man must now adapt to the age of technology by keeping his body fit and supple through means other than work.

In 1700, Dr. Bernadino Ramazzini, the father of occupational medicine, wrote a book, *De Morbis Artificiam* or *The Diseases of Workers.* In this important text, a synthesis of all knowledge on occupational disease up to the end of the 17th century, Dr. Ramazzini observed, noted, and came to conclusions about the diseases that affected labourers in certain occupations. His descriptions of illnesses occuring at that time in farmers, fishermen, and miners were very accurate and are applicable even in our time.

"Various and manifold," he wrote, "is the harvest of diseases reaped by certain workers from crafts and trades they pursue... I ascribed certain violent and uncertain emotions and unnatural positions of the body by reason of which the natural substitute of the vital machine is so impaired that serious disease gradually develops."

Although he attributed many types of diseases to heavy manual labour, it was only in sedentary occupations that Dr. Ramazzini found sciatica and back trouble. "Tailors are often subject to numbness of the legs, lameness and sciatica," he wrote. "They work at their job and become bent, humpbacked and hold their head down like people looking for something on the ground. This is the effect of their sedentary life and the bent posture of their body as they sit and apply themselves all day to their tasks in the shops where they sew.

"All sedentary workers suffer from lumbago," Ramazzini wrote, advising these workers "to take physical exercise at any rate on their holidays. Let them make the best use they can of Sunday, and to some extent counteract the harm done by many days of sedentary life."

It is interesting that so many people still believe that backache is due to excessive work when even centuries ago physicians noted that backache plagued those who worked at sedentary occupations. As most of us spend our time sitting down on the job in this automated age it becomes obvious why backache is an ever-increasing problem.

Back at Work

True or false?: The majority of workers with back problems have jobs involving physical labour.

The incidence of back pain is the *same* for those in light office work as for those whose jobs involve heavy labour. This fact must come as a surprise after my previous statements about the need to exercise the back muscles. Hard physical labour should give the back muscles the workout they need to keep the back in shape, but this would only be the case if a job required constant physical exertion. In western society, however, the majority of laborers have jobs requiring only intermittent or sporadic heavy work; as a result, this group has a high incidence of back pain. A truck driver, for example, who sits for most of the day and then unloads his vehicle at the end of a long trip is a prime candidate for backache.

While there is no difference in the *incidence* of back pain between the two groups of workers (light vs. heavy work), there is, however, a difference in the *effect* of back pain on the two groups. Obviously, a worker engaged in hard physical labour will not be able to return to the job as quickly as an employee who has less physically demanding duties. We have found in some companies that laborers who have just returned to work after a two-or three-week vacation or layoff seem more susceptible to back problems because of the loss of physical fitness. Doctors, often unaware of the job demands a patient faces, predicate a return to work on *absence of pain. Back fitness,* or the ability to perform tasks should, instead, be the indicator. If these are not taken into account, the worker could, and probably will, develop back pain again.

There is yet another difference in how the two kinds of workers are affected by back pain. For the laborer, backache is a more emotionally loaded problem than for the office worker. The laborer tends to be more frightened of the pain because he views his back as his "power house." If it doesn't function properly there could be a significant threat to his financial security.

The hard-driving executive is a prime candidate for backache. Bad postural habits at the desk where the executive often works long hours, tension that contracts the muscles of the back and causes a reduced blood supply, finished off by a weekend of competitive sports, will often culminate in backache due to muscle spasm. This type of worker is actually in the same position as the truck driver: intermittent physical activity after long hours of sedentary work can bring this weekend athlete groaning to the doctor with a severe muscle sprain in the lower back.

Backs Are Like
Fine Wines

True or false?: Back problems are rare before the age of 30.

Let's begin by examining a table in *Manual Lifting and Related Fields* by the Labour Safety Council of Ontario, Canada.

Age Distribution Of						
Back Injuries (1979)						
Age in years:	-20	21-30	31-40	41-50	51-60	61+
Percentage of back injuries:	6.4%	26.5%	31.2%	21.5%	11.4%	3%

As you can see, back problems are *not* rare before the age of 30. There is a high incidence of low back injuries in people who are in the prime of life. Where the difference lies, however, is in the severity of the back complaints of the two groups, aged 21 to 30 and 31 to 40. In the younger group the pain of backache tends to be less severe than in the older group and it also disappears more quickly. Because there is less long-term disability there is less time taken off work by the younger group. In the older group the functional loss and disability is greater, leading to more time away from work and higher costs for surgery and disability pensions. That's why back pain is commonly considered a degenerative disease that attacks the older person. In reality, back pain is a major—and basically unappreciated—problem for young adults. While the "problem" backs occur at a later age, the disease process begins much earlier. The seeds are being sown for the recurring bouts of backache that can make life miserable during our most productive years.

In an article, "Backache in Boys—A New Problem," V.A. Grantham, the medical officer for Oundle School in Northamptonshire, England, states his belief "that the number of boys developing backache is increasing among boys aged 13 to 15 years." He conjectures that this could be in part due to an increased athletic program, which puts a greater number of boys at risk. He also believes that after an injury the boys are returned to games too soon—before their backs are totally fit and have been strengthened by proper exercise. I agree with his thinking on the subject, but I believe there could be another reason as well: there is a tendency among teenagers today to affect a slouching posture that can lead to weakened back muscles with resulting problems in later life. In Chapter 9, I explain how bad posture affects the back.

If you have had an occasional backache but have shrugged it off as unimportant, remember that pain in the back is a signal that all is not well.

Occasional bouts of backache in your young adult life may well lead to a "problem" back in your thirties and forties.

There is, however, one comforting fact about our backs and aging. If you look back at the table you will see that the problems tend to lessen as we get older. Nature has seen to it that our backs, like fine wine, get better with age.

Back in
the Doghouse

True or false?: Human beings suffer from back problems because of their upright posture.

A popular belief holds that our back problems are partly the result of the evolutionary process from quadruped to biped. It is undoubtedly true that humans' upright posture makes the lower back vulnerable to strains and injuries, but the question remains: why are there people who, despite a lifetime of heavy manual labour, never have a backache?

There's no question that the upright posture produces significant compressive and shearing forces on the discs and vertebrae in the spine. There is also no question that the back is a delicate, intricate, and balanced mechanism. The point is, however, that if you mistreat and weaken this mechanism you will have problems. Treat it correctly and keep it in shape, and you will have a back that never gives you a moment's trouble.

By the way, there's no need to envy our four-footed friends. They are not all immune to back problems. Any veterinarian will tell you that some dogs also have disc trouble and while lumbar disc protrusion in man predominantly causes pain it's far worse for dogs—in them the disc protrusion causes paralysis.

It's also interesting to note that disc disease is less frequent in the sporting dog than in the house pet. It appears that a dog needs exercise to keep its back fit, just like the two-footed master.

A Back
Like Alice

True or false?: Women suffer from backache more than men.

The incidence of backache is the same for both sexes but there is a particularly vulnerable period in women's lives—pregnancy. Women usually work at jobs requiring less heavy labour than men and in many cases pregnancy is the only time their spines are challenged by a heavy load.

Why do pregnant women become so susceptible to back pain? Again, let's think about posture and muscles. Picture a woman five months pregnant. The forward load she is carrying in her abdomen has produced a swayback condition in her spine, which weakens the back muscles so they become fatigued more easily. That muscle fatigue brings stress to the lower part of the spine. If her back muscles were weak before pregnancy, due to faulty posture and lack of exercise, the additional strain placed on them during pregnancy will cause pain—a nagging backache at first, then more pain as the pregnancy progresses.

At this point let me quickly reassure any woman who might be viewing a future pregnancy with alarm. There is absolutely no need to endure backache during pregnancy. Proper conditioning exercises before pregnancy (and during, but only on the advice of your obstetrician) will enable you to sail happily through the nine months with nary a twinge.

Exercises after pregnancy are essential to recondition the abdomen and back muscles and most doctors so advise new mothers. This is an especially vulnerable time for a woman's back, since she will be so totally involved with her new infant, lifting, bending, and carrying. Reconditioning her weakened muscles at this time could help prevent a lifetime of chronic backache.

When there's an incompatability between the demands and loads placed on the spine and the capability of the spine to withstand them, it doesn't matter a hoot whether you're a man or a woman—the result, for both sexes, will be a backache.

Back to Haunt You

True or false?: If you've had occasional back problems and they go away, there's no need to worry.

Most people consider a backache a single, unrelated entity, somewhat like catching a cold. This is partly because of the short duration of the pain and the long intervals between attacks.

However, as you are discovering, low back pain is usually part of a recurrent disease process with each subsequent backache tending to be more severe, to last longer, and to be more disabling than the last. These acute episodes are usually interspersed with relatively pain-free periods, perhaps marked by morning stiffness and occasional discomfort. The process usually begins in young adulthood and much too frequently culminates in middle age with chronic unremitting pain, severe disability, or surgery.

Again, when patients are unaware of how the back functions, they logically respond to each back episode by reducing the demands of life — such as sports, hobbies, or work—in the expectation that future problems will be prevented. Ian MacNab, a noted Canadian back surgeon, has called the aching back "a malevolent dictator robbing the individual of the full enjoyment of life."

Don't ignore those early attacks of low back pain—they are a signal from your back. It is trying to tell you that all is not well.

The Camel's Back

True or false?: Backaches are usually caused by lifting something the wrong way.

It is human nature to want to attribute a problem to something definite, something we can come to grips with and avoid in the future. That's why almost all back sufferers will say that their backaches happened because they lifted something awkwardly. Now there's no doubt that lifting objects the right way will reduce the hazards of back pain. In fact, later in the book I will devote an entire chapter to proper lifting techniques. But what I want to emphasize here is that a lifting episode, in many cases, was simply the straw that broke the camel's back: the back problem was likely beginning long before that particular mishap.

To illustrate my point I would like to show you what an examination of statistics from the Ontario Workman's Compensation Board revealed. The predominant type of low back injury among workers was attributed to over-exertion, which means that the employee's back was too weak to handle a task or, conversely, that the task was too great even for the employee with a strong back. It turned out that 62 per cent of low back injuries fell into that category, while the other 38 per cent were caused by falling objects, slips or falls, and unknown causes. Further questioning showed that only 26 per cent of the employees in the over-exertion classification actually hurt their backs lifting an object. The others could not give a definite cause for their backache. Backaches are not *usually* caused, as we would like to think, by lifting something the wrong way. In 80 per cent of cases backaches are caused by overworked muscles that rebel against strain by going into sustained contraction or spasm.

Backing Out
of Work

True or false?: Back pain is the second leading cause of absenteeism in industry after the common cold.

Colds and flu remain the number one cause of absenteeism but it should give us pause when we are told that back pain comes second. If this doesn't convince you that backache is reaching epidemic proportions in North America, I don't know what will.

If the pain is caused by muscle strain, as is usually the case, doctors almost universally recommend bed rest and medication. They know that the best healer of all is time, and that the pain caused by most back strains will disappear in approximately three weeks no matter what is done. Unfortunately, when the pain disappears, most people tend to think the back is once again in good shape. They don't realize that an injured back is never completely cured unless steps are taken to recondition the weakened muscles. The National Back Fitness Test in this book now gives you the opportunity to test your back after a muscle strain has healed. The results of the test will show just what condition your back is in and what steps can be taken to remedy it.

They Shoot Backs, Don't They?

True or false?: X rays are essential to help determine the cause of backache.

It's true that with a serious backache, an X ray film of the back is part of the process by which a physician rules out diseases such as cancer, abscesses, inflammation, tuberculosis, ankylosing spondylitis, osteoporosis, Paget's disease, Scheuermann's disease, or spondylosis. Collectively, these diseases account for an insignificant percentage of back ailments but, nonetheless, it is important that a diagnosis be made because a specific treatment may be required.

However, patients who have been diagnosed as having common low back pain tend to over-emphasize the importance of X rays. I can assure you that once serious disease has been ruled out, an X ray tells the doctor very little. Dr. Ian MacNab, a world-recognized authority on modern back surgery, explains in his book, *Backache,* that because of the difficulties in diagnosing low back pain there was a period when clinicians laid the blame for inexplicable symptoms on the diverse and curious anomalies of the back revealed on an X ray. When it was later discovered that these anatomical variants occurred just as frequently in the population at large as in those with backache, it was evident that they could not be the sole cause of low back pain.

How often have you heard someone say, "My X ray showed a spinal defect that is causing my backache," or "My backache is caused by a degenerating disc which showed up on an X ray." Yet Dr. MacNab has pointed out that a study of the X rays of 300 laborers showed *no difference* in the incidence of degenerative changes in the spines, although 150 complained of backache and were under treatment while the other 150 had no history of low back pain. The fact is that degenerative disc disease, a normal part of the aging process, begins in all of us after 25.

An X ray also serves to depress some patients when everything on it appears normal. "Why do I have such awful pain if my X ray is normal?" the patient asks. Again, let's remember that a muscle in spasm and the resultant deep swelling of the tissue *doesn't* show up on an X ray film. Another unfortunate aspect of an X ray is that it causes people to over-emphasize the importance of the bones in the spine while neglecting to consider the equally critical part played by the muscles of the back.

It would be wise for both patient and doctor alike to keep in mind what Dr. MacNab has written on the subject of X rays: "The first question a physician must ask himself when he has recognized an anatomical abnormality on X ray is "I wonder what is the cause of this patient's backache?"

Back to the Dictionary

True or false?: A "slipped disc" is the reason for most back pain.

Although there is, in reality, no such thing as a "slipped disc," the term has become part of modern usage. There are many synonyms that doctors prefer, including herniated disc, prolapsed disc, bulging disc, sequestrated disc, soft disc, protruding disc, ruptured disc, and extruded disc. Doctors prefer these other terms because there is no way a disc, which is a shock absorber separating the vertebrae, can actually slip out of place. It merely bulges when there is too much pressure on the spine; when it bulges enough to come into contact with a nerve and causes pain, the condition is colloquially referred to as a "slipped disc."

This occurs in less than five per cent of backaches seen in a general practice and is diagnosed by a doctor when the following conditions exist: the patient complains of pain radiating down into the leg and this pain is coupled with changes in the nerve outflow tracks to the lower extremities indicated by muscle weakness. As well, during an examination, the patient may be unable to raise the leg or there may be changes of sensation in the leg, such as numbness, tingling, or loss of reflex in the knee or ankle. Even more serious, there may be loss of tone in the muscle sphincters in the bladder and bowel and loss of sensation in the rectal area, which is a medical emergency requiring immediate treatment. Fortunately, it's extremely rare.

No conclusive diagnosis of a herniated disc can be made from a plain X ray. Unless a myelogram, venogram, or other sophisticated testing is done, no doctor can make a diagnosis of a so-called slipped disc. These tests sometimes become necessary when a patient's pain cannot be relieved by conservative treatment over a period of weeks or when there is increasing loss of nerve function in the extremities.

A herniated disc is usually a progressive condition, first starting with mild discomfort in the lower back due to increased weakening of the tissue over a period of years. In most cases, the herniated disc is not the beginning of back trouble but the final stage of a process in which the warning signs have been ignored. It is simply the end result of a system that has been out of balance for a number of years.

The Running Back

True or false?: If you regularly play an active sport, you will not develop a back problem.

It's true that active sports do give some immunity to back problems but the operative word in the statement is *regularly*. Those who have allowed their back muscles to become weak and out of condition are often asking for trouble when they play weekend sports. The Monday morning backache syndrome is a signal that the back was unable to keep up with unusual activity on the weekend.

Do you love jogging? It's terrific for a strong back but can play havoc with a weak one. The good news is that you do have a choice—either give up sport if it bothers your back or improve the capability of your back so you can continue to enjoy it.

After you have tried the National Back Fitness Test and have graded your performance, you will be better equipped to determine which sports to play and which to avoid while you are in the process of reconditioning your back. Once it is strong, you will probably be able to play the sport you most enjoy and have more fun at it because you'll be in better shape. Remember, however, that you can't bank fitness. Your back is the foundation of bodily movement, the key to all activity and it demands *regular* exercise to maintain fitness and suppleness.

Cutbacks

True or false?: If you get a serious back problem, surgical repair will fix it up permanently.

Surgery for serious back problems is not the cure-all that people dream of. It is the answer to only a fraction of back problems in which a specific mechanical condition exists—a bulging disc pressing against a nerve, for example. And even then it is only one step in what will be a lifelong process of back care.

There was a time when surgery was held to be a panacea for back problems. But the results were so often discouraging that in the last decade it was not uncommon to meet patients who had had two, three, or four operations and still suffered backache. Their lack of success at permanently relieving backache has made surgeons much less enthusiastic about operations during recent years. In the United States, surgery fails completely in about 20 per cent of cases, and three out of five patients continue to have symptoms despite it.

Just the same, a patient who is constantly suffering from severe back pain hopes desperately that an operation will permanently relieve the agony. The pain indicates to patients that something needs to be fixed and they believe the surgeon has the tools to accomplish the repair. When told that surgery will not relieve most chronic pain, patients feel that they have been left in a vacuum. This book was written to help fill that vacuum.

3

Muscle Spasm: Why It Hurts and What to Do About It

"It is more important to know what sort of person has a disease than to know what sort of disease a person has," Hippocrates pointed out. When a patient presents himself in a doctor's office complaining of a backache, the great Greek physician's statement is one that all medical practitioners must constantly bear in mind. The case history offered by the patient gives the doctor as many clues to the nature of the illness as the medical examination. Why? Because backache, unlike tonsillitis, is not a clear-cut problem. The pain in your back can be the signal for a variety of diseases and yet in most cases there are few significant physical signs for the doctor to observe. As I mentioned earlier, 90 per cent of the time, the backache is going to be due to a musculo-skeletal disorder—or, in layman's language, muscle spasm. The doctor, while being aware that this is the likely cause of the pain, also knows that the patient is feeling anxious and distressed. The doctor is also pretty certain that the patient, a product of the speeded-up 20th century, is going to expect a fast, definite diagnosis with an equally rapid and definite cure.

Now, despite the mythology, doctors are human: they like to live up to a patient's expectations. If the patient wants an impressive medical term to account for the distress, the doctor will often try to give one—usually something vague and indefinite that will cover the problem. "You have degenerative disc disease," the doctor will authoritatively inform the back sufferer, who turns pale. No wonder I'm in such pain, the patient thinks as a vision of the discs crumbling like stale cookies flashes to mind. The doctor's attempt to satisfy the patient's need for a diagnosis has unwittingly created fear and has also set up a situation where there is a terrific

31

possibility for misinterpretation. If another doctor later tells the patient that he or she has arthritis of the spine, which simply means an inflammation of the joints, the patient becomes even more fearful and distrustful, and may scurry off to the latest miracle worker. As I noted earlier, the backache will probably go away in three weeks no matter what treatment is given. Thus the last person who treated the patient will be credited with the cure. Of course, because there often is no permanent cure, the patient will continue to have backaches, and that's the pity of it all.

You can see why the nature of the communication between the patient with a backache and the doctor is such an important part of the healing process. The casual use of technical language can throw the patient into such a tailspin that the healing process cannot be effectively carried out. A doctor, then, must take pains to explain the back problem as simply and clearly as possible, and should also keep in mind that most patients equate pain with harm. If the backache is severe, they are likely to think that they have a disease equally severe.

The patient's presentation of his or her history and symptoms not only provides the necessary information to make a medical diagnosis, it also reveals to the physician the patient's view of the problem and underlying fears. Unless those anxieties are fully grasped by the doctor, it is unlikely the patient will co-operate with the simple treatment for common backache that is usually most effective.

My back-care practice is predicated on the belief that the doctor must not only tell the patient what is wrong, but what the diagnosis means, what it could develop into, and why certain treatments are prescribed.

I'd like to show you, through the experiences of a patient, why a case history is so important, how and why the examination is conducted, what it reveals, and why the treatment prescribed is necessary.

The Story of Margaret N.
Age 35

I'm divorced and I have three children, aged 7, 8, and 10. Their father pays child support but it isn't quite enough to keep us safe from galloping inflation. Last year I decided that I would eventually have to get a job and that unless I went back to school for some training I'd never be able to qualify for work that paid a decent wage. I applied to journalism school, was accepted and I just finished my first year exams last month.

I was fantastically lucky: through a friend, I was offered a job on a magazine three months ago and even though it meant studying for my exams all night and working all day, I *grabbed* it. Jobs on magazines are hard to land and it was a heaven-sent opportunity.

The kids have been terrific—I mean, they hardly have a mother right now but we do all the housework together on weekends; and I told them it was one way we can keep the house from total disintegration and spend some time together too. Anyhow, there's not enough money for a housekeeper until I begin earning more. That'll take a couple of years, I'm afraid, but we'll manage somehow. I do want a full-time housekeeper eventually to look after the kids. They're still too young to be alone so much and I worry about them constantly.

My job is very demanding. Friday nights we put the magazine to bed and I don't get out of the office until 9 or 10 o'clock. My next-door neighbor babysits for me that evening. She's a terrific woman and I'd be lost without her. She's like a second mother to me—my mother died a few years ago of cancer of the pancreas. I miss her terribly but I was glad when she finally died—the cancer had spread to her spine and she was in unbearable pain.

I must admit that the last three months have been exhausting and just as I was beginning to think everything was easing up because the exams were finally over, I developed this backache. I've never had anything so miserable in my life. The pain is excruciating and it never goes away.

I went to my family doctor three weeks ago and he took an X ray but nothing showed up on it, so he gave me tranquillizers. I hate them—I hardly ever take an aspirin and here I am loaded to the gills with pills and tranquillizers. I'm walking into walls at work and it's hard for me to think and do my job properly with all this stuff zapping my brain. It's not as if the stuff has got rid of the pain. It never leaves me for a second, and it's especially bad when I'm sitting and I have to sit all day at my desk. I can't take time off work—there's no one to replace me and, since I've only been there three months, I'm afraid I'd lose my job. But it's getting to the point where I don't think I can stand one more day like this. It's far worse than the backache I had during my last pregnancy. I had a backache all through it but the obstetrician told me it was to be expected. My daughter was born very quickly after my son and my back never got the chance to return to normal because I was pregnant again so quickly. The third pregnancy was a nightmare—I was sick all the time and my husband and I were not getting along (our marriage was a mess; we separated two years later, actually). The backache disappeared after my daughter was born and I've only had one other attack of back pain. Last year I was helping the house painter carry a rug out of the living room and my back gave out for a few days but the pain disappeared fairly quickly so I never bothered about it.

My GP sent me to a neurologist last week but he couldn't find any serious problem and then a woman I work with advised me to come and see you. So here I am. I hope you can fix my back quickly. I already feel guilty about taking so much time off work to see so many doctors.

Even if the woman sitting across from me hadn't mentioned that she was in pain it would have been obvious. Perched uncomfortably on the edge of her chair, her lifeless face and the monotone in which she spoke showed that three weeks of debilitating pain had created not only fatigue but depression as well. I explained to her that I would need to make an examination and asked her to put on a gown and wait for me in the examining room. "I'm glad I wore a skirt today," she said when I entered. "I'd have never been able to pull slacks off. I even had to ask your nurse to help me off with my shoes."

"This examination won't take long—about ten minutes," I said. "While you're standing I'd like you to tell me when your backache began, show me where the pain started, where it is now, and where it has spread." Patients are understandably vague about anatomy and when they tell you they have a back pain it could be located anywhere from the top of the back down to the buttocks. I also ask my patients to show me whether the pain is in the front or back of the thighs and whether it radiates down to or below the knee. Their answers offer clues that help determine whether the patient is suffering from referred pain or whether the pain is due to nerve root irritation in the spine.

A doctor also needs to know which activities influence the pain. "Sitting is awful," Margaret told me. "Getting up is even worse." But she admitted that resting in bed did ease the pain somewhat.

Because back pain is a symptom and not a disease, the source of the pain may lie outside the spine. Although this occurs in only a small percentage of cases it is for that reason a doctor asks back patients like Margaret for the family history of disease as well as other questions relating to changes in the bowels or in the appetite, abnormal bleeding, weight loss, and chronic coughing.

While Margaret was standing in the examining room I had been observing her overall posture. I wanted to see whether her spine was straight or tilted to one side, whether she favored one side of her body more than another and whether there was a sag in one buttock. I had also asked her to walk around while I noted any abnormality in her stride and how much the movement bothered her. She was also asked to bend forward and backward and to the side, so that I could once again see how much the pain limited her movements.

Once she was on the examining table, I determined her knee and ankle reflexes by tapping the tendons with a reflex hammer. The next step was to assess the patient's muscle power by asking her to perform certain tests. The most important of these are straight leg raises to see if the sciatic nerve is involved; if so, a possible disc disorder is indicated. Another test—bending both knees and drawing them up to the chest—can indicate low back strain or spasm if there is pain when it is performed. I then checked the sensations in her lower legs by pricking them with a pin to see if the nerve function was intact.

While she was lying on her stomach I checked her buttocks for muscle tone and sensation and palpated her back, searching for spasm and tenderness. I also examined her spine for any lumps or tenderness or an abnormal curvature. A rectal examination was also conducted to check for growths, swellings, and the position of the cervix, and to evaluate the condition of the coccyx. If the patient were a man, I would be checking the prostate gland, a possible location for concern. Finally, the organs in the abdominal cavity were checked for enlargement, and blood and urine samples were taken. I then looked over her X rays and, as she had told me, they showed no abnormalities.

The examination was now over and I asked Margaret to get dressed and come back to my office. There I explained to her the reason for the examination: to rule out the small percentage of serious diseases that fall into two categories—significant *congenital* disease (which means a disease one is born with, such as congenital scoliosis) or *acquired* disease (under which fall osteoporosis, ankylosing spondylitis, tuberculosis, and tumours).

I would like at this point to stress that this book is not intended to be used for self-diagnosis. Although the majority of backaches are due to musculo-skeletal disorders, anyone suffering from a backache that is progressively getting worse or lingering on for a week or two should be examined by a doctor in order to rule out possible serious disease.

As I had suspected Margaret showed no signs of cancer or other pathology. I noticed her sigh of relief when I told her this and I was not surprised, for I was sure her mother's death had been preying on her mind more than she would care to admit. It's quite natural for anyone who has seen a relative or friend die because of a tumour in the spine to be apprehensive about a backache.

My other concern, as I explained to her, was to make sure she did not have a herniated disc, because this condition, if left untreated, can cause irreversible damage to the nerves and muscles of the legs and feet. As there was no evidence of a herniated disc, I told Margaret that she had the most common back disorder of all: back pain due to musculo-skeletal sprain or, in layman's language, muscle spasm, which had produced tenderness and loss of function in the lower lumbar vertebrae.

Margaret found it hard to believe that a spasm could be the main reason for her pain. "Surely," she suggested, "there must be something else happening in my back. I can't believe that one muscle could make me feel this awful for such a length of time."

However, in Margaret's case, it wasn't just one muscle that had gone into spasm. I explained to her that, in a sense, muscle spasm is a protective mechanism that happens when a muscle or joint is injured and under excessive strain. Sometimes nearby muscles also contract in an effort to splint the injured area and prevent further damage to it. That is what had happened in Margaret's back.

"Margaret, have you ever had a night cramp in your leg?" I asked.

"Sure," she said. "They're very painful."

"Well, just try to imagine a muscle in your back contracted in the same way," I said. "Contracted muscles can become very tender and painful when they are swollen by the constant tension of spasm. The pain of spasm results because of a lack of nutrition in the muscle. Blood with its oxygen and nutrients comes in to the muscles through arteries and leaves through veins carrying with it metabolic waste products. When a muscle contracts for a long period due to spasm, oxygen and nutrients cannot reach the muscle cells because the capillaries, tiny vessels lying between the arteries and veins, are squeezed shut. It's these capillaries through which the oxygen and waste move from blood to the muscle. The waste products can produce pain when they accumulate in the muscle and the lack of oxygen also causes the muscle tissue to hurt.

"Margaret," I said, "make the strongest fist you can and keep holding it."

After a few seconds she said, "It's beginning to get tired."

"Keep holding it," I said.

"Hey, it's becoming uncomfortable," she finally said.

"Okay, release it. I just wanted to demonstrate how any muscle contracted for a longer period of time than is normal will begin to get tired and then hurt."

"But why does a muscle go into spasm in the first place?" Margaret asked.

"Muscle spasm can be triggered by a number of factors. An injury, excessive demand placed on the muscle, or emotional tension can cause a spasm, especially when the muscles are weak. In your case, I think it's been a combination of factors—excessive demand and emotional tension."

"Well, what do I do to get rid of it?"

Like most patients Margaret was surprised to hear that complete bedrest was the only way her backache would get better. "This advice is not given lightly," I told her. "If I had seen you three weeks ago I might have advised a conservative medical treatment that consisted of heat therapy, pain killers, and limited activity. But your back condition is getting worse and complete bedrest is essential when a back isn't getting any better. If you won't agree to stay home in bed I'd advise hospitalization."

One look at Margaret's face and I could tell that even if she agreed to bedrest she would remain skeptical. I was not surprised by her reaction. This was one tough lady who had been hanging in through a lot of bad times. Like many of my patients, bedrest was the last thing she wanted and the least acceptable. In an era of fast-working miracle drugs, bedrest seems much too simple and far too slow a treatment. I decided that further explanation was necessary if I was to obtain her whole-hearted co-operation.

"If you had a sprained ankle," I asked, "would you be surprised to hear that you could not walk around on it till the inflammation died down?" She shook her head. "That's because you would be able to see the swelling in your ankle and that would convince you that you had to take weight off the ankle so it could heal properly. The injured muscles or joints in your back that are helping to support the spine cannot rest unless you lie down and take weight off the spine. While you are standing or moving you are forcing the muscles to work because they must defy gravity. They will not heal while you are forcing them to work beyond their present capacity."

"Okay, you've made your point. How long will I have to stay in bed?"

"I think a week should be more than adequate," I told her.

"A week! A whole week! I'll lose my job!"

"Ask your employer to phone me and I'll gladly explain the need for your week off. I doubt you'll have any trouble once they know why I have recommended this course."

"Can I get up to make the children's meals?"

"No, I want you to have complete bedrest. The only time you can get up is to go to the bathroom and our physiotherapist is going to show you how to accomplish that with the least amount of effort and discomfort. You can direct the children from bed. It will probably mean a lot of soup and sandwiches, I'm afraid, but you've been worrying because you don't see much of them. Here's your chance."

"It's going to be awfully hard for me to lie in bed for a whole week, especially when I know how much work will be waiting for me after I get up."

"That's why I want you to stay on the tranquillizers for a few more days," I told her. "They will make you feel sleepier and more relaxed so that staying in bed will be easier for you. As soon as you begin to feel better—let's say in two or three days—you can discontinue the tranquillizers and any pain medication you no longer need. Now I'm going to take you in to meet my physiotherapist. She's going to spend a few minutes with you and show you how to rest your spine in what we call the neutral position. She's also going to give you some practical information on back

37

care so you will understand why lying in a certain way will put your back in the optimum position for healing. I want to see you in one week's time and I'm sure you'll be feeling a lot better by then. When things completely settle down, I'll have you try our back fitness test. If the results of the test confirm my suspicions about the condition of your back muscles, you've got some work to do. We're going to show you how to strengthen your back to prevent future episodes of back pain."

4

How Your Back Works

The back, for most people, is a deep, dark secret. It's the plodding workhorse of the body, ignored while it steadily does its job. But when it breaks down, it becomes of all-consuming interest: back problems can, after all, partially, sometimes completely, immobilize us. What's more, they hurt. And we can't even see why the back hurts. When we painfully and slowly twist around to examine it in a mirror, it looks just the same, even though it has forced us to limp around, tilted to one side like a drunken sailor, one hand vainly pressed to the spot where it aches. What is even more frustrating is that the pain goes on and on and on. When we have a toothache we expect a quick visit to a dentist will relieve the pain fairly rapidly. Why on earth, then, can't a doctor fix a backache just as quickly?

Dealing as I do with thousands of back problems every year, I am very aware of my patients' frustration. Many of them are much like Margaret in the previous chapter, hard-driving personalities with a grin-and-bear-it attitude toward illness. I know that unless they are given a demonstration of how the back works and why it acts and reacts in certain ways, their co-operation in the prescribed treatment will be difficult to get. My back practice is, therefore, predicated on the belief that an informed patient will be a co-operative and relaxed one. And that in itself will help the back heal much more quickly.

With this in mind, I introduce patients like Margaret to my sister, Jan, our in-house physiotherapist. She, in turn, always introduces them to another member of our staff, "Skinny" the skeleton, who resides in her office and plays an invaluable part in the back education of our patients.

One of the first things Jan points out is that, because Skinny is just a collection of the bones making up the human body, he must hang suspended from a bar. We tend to forget that without the support given to our bones by the tendons, muscles, and ligaments, we too would fall in a heap. Skinny serves to remind the patient that the bones of the back are only part of the total picture. The bones, like Skinny, are static and lifeless. The muscles are the dynamic part of the body; they make humans living, moving creatures.

A lot of our patients are rather apprehensive when they see what a large collection of bones go to make up the back. "I don't see how I can possibly learn all about the spine," Margaret said after eyeing Skinny for a few moments. "He looks like a rather complicated fellow."

"Don't worry," I said. "We're not going to subject you to the kind of detailed anatomy course a medical student would be given. The physiotherapist is going to spend just a few minutes showing you the working anatomy of the spine. It will help you to understand why resting in certain positions will help your spine to heal. You'll also learn why the muscles of your back must be kept in good condition. This will be one anatomy lesson that will pay big dividends for your future health."

Let's join Margaret in the following simple anatomy lesson, because the first step toward a problem-free back is the knowledge of how it works.

The Spinal Column

The spinal column is a marvel of biological engineering, providing both strength and stability along with movement and flexibility to the body. Basically, the spine has three main functions:

1. It's the body's principal scaffolding, supporting the skull and anchoring ribs, pelvis, and shoulder bones.
2. It provides broad, boney areas for the attachment of the muscles, tendons, and ligaments that permit the body's movement.
3. It houses the spinal cord, the vital cable linking the brain to all other parts of the body.

The spinal column has a double-S shape and is comprised of 33 small and generally flat bones, called vertebrae, sitting one on top of the other from the neck to the base of the spine. The spine itself can be divided into five regions:

The cervical spine

1. This region consists of the seven upper vertebrae, which support the head and allow the neck to move to the right and left. I like to

THE SPINAL COLUMN

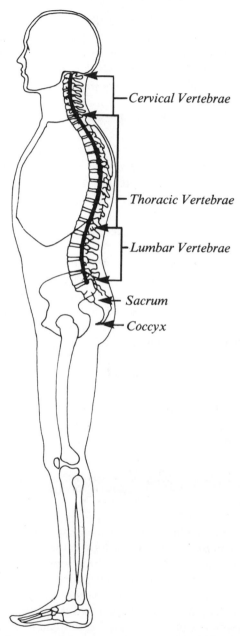

Cervical Vertebrae

Thoracic Vertebrae

Lumbar Vertebrae

Sacrum

Coccyx

think of these vertebrae as the "yes" and "no" bones, because they allow us to nod "yes", and shake our heads "no".

The thoracic spine

2. There are 12 vertebrae forming this area of the spine and each of them is attached to two ribs, forming a rib cage to protect the vital organs—the heart and lungs. Because the ribs in turn are connected to the sternum or breastbone, which is relatively rigid, these vertebrae are quite stable and not very mobile.

The lumbar spine

3. The five large vertebrae that form this section of the spine in the lower back are broader and heavier than the vertebrae above since they have to support the large mass of the upper body. These lower vertebrae allow our bodies to bend forward and backward.

The sacrum

4. The sacrum consists of five separate bones that are formed during the development of the foetus and finally fuse to form a single, immobile structure. This broad, triangular structure is attached at the top to the lumbar section and on the sides to the pelvis, forming the solid boney pelvic ring, which is very strong and relatively immune to injury.

The coccyx

5. This collection of four small bones at the base of the spine is commonly referred to as the tailbone. The coccyx rarely gives us trouble unless, of course, we fall on it.

The Vertebrae and Discs

Just as the spine is a marvel of biological engineering, so, in turn, are each of the parts that comprise it. Let's now look at the lumbar vertebrae, rather complicated bones designed for three functions: weight-bearing, movement, and protection of the delicate spinal cord. Because a realistic drawing of a vertebra is quite confusing for a patient, our physiotherapist draws a simple working diagram on her chalk board. Depicting the major portion of the vertebra, which is the solid, thick, and broad part of the bone at the front or anterior part of the spine. She draws a square and points out to the patient that this portion of the vertebra has been designed to bear weight.

Between the solid part of each vertebra is a disc. The physiotherapist explains that a disc is composed of a capsule of layered ligament, the *annulus fibrosus,* enclosing a jelly-like fluid known as the *nucleus pulposus.* The discs that separate each vertebra act like shock absorbers for the spine, compressing when weight is put upon it and springing back to their original shape when the weight is taken away. If the spine were without discs, the vertebrae would grind against one another and quickly wear out. Not only do the discs serve to separate the vertebrae, they also act as a

NORMAL VERTEBRAE AND DISC

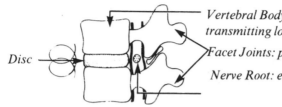

Vertebral Body: strongly constructed for transmitting loads through the spine

Facet Joints: permit movement

Nerve Root: exists from the spinal cord

Disc

NORMAL VERTEBRAE AND DISC REACTING TO SPINAL LOADING

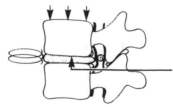

Under the weight of a load the disc compresses like a spring ready to return to its original position when the load is removed

hydraulic system, their gelatinous interiors dispersing pressure on the spine evenly in all directions along the back.

At the back or posterior part of the vertebrae are the facet joints. Called synovial because they permit movement, the delicate facet joints are linked to the solid weight-bearing front part of the vertebrae by boney bridges. These bridges, fitting neatly into one another, form a continuous tunnel of bone enclosing and protecting the spinal cord.

The spinal cord is a transmission cable that carries the impulses and messages from the brain to all parts of the body through nerve roots emerging from each side of it at the level of each vertebra along the spine. Now, when you look at the diagram, you can see why a prolapsed or herniated disc bulging into the small space called the *intervertebral fora-men* can exert pressure on the nerve root and cause pain and injury to the nerve.

THE LUMBAR VERTEBRAE ARE DESIGNED
FOR WEIGHT-BEARING AND MOVEMENT

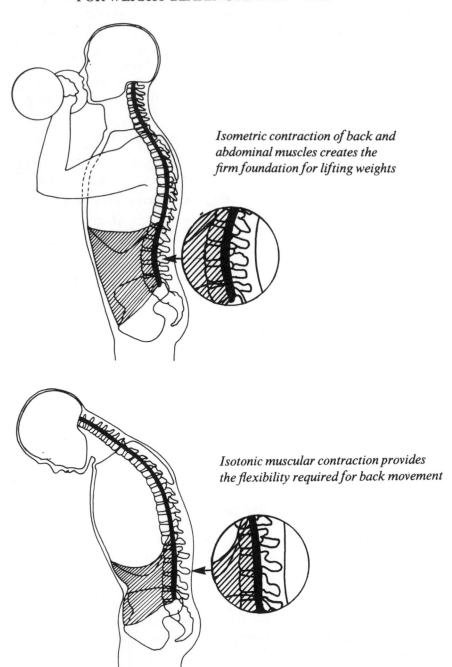

Isometric contraction of back and
abdominal muscles creates the
firm foundation for lifting weights

Isotonic muscular contraction provides
the flexibility required for back movement

The Working Unit
of the Back

I am now going to focus on the five lumbar vertebrae and how they work. Why? Because these vertebrae in the lower back are the trouble-makers that cause most backaches. If you recall the thoracic or chest region of the spine, you'll remember that the vertebrae there are attached to the ribs and form a relatively rigid cage, which is structurally strong. Conversely, the lower part of the spine, the lumbar area, is designed for movement, although it too must bear weight. When you see a dancer or gymnast bending and twisting gracefully, it's the lumbar vertebrae that allow such movement. Yet this lower part of the spine also lets a dancer stand and hold a partner aloft. While wonderfully designed for weight-bearing and movement, the lower vertebrae cannot move and bear weight at the same time. It's these contradictory abilities that make the lumbar vertebrae so susceptible to injury. I will have much more to say about this in a later chapter dealing with bending and lifting.

Stacked one on top of another, the five lumbar vertebrae form a column of bone working in concert to permit forward and backward bending. This working unit sits on a firm foundation called the pelvic platform. Just as the mast of a ship is attached to the deck by guy wires, so the lower vertebrae are attached to the pelvis by ligaments and muscles.

The pelvis is a bone made up of three solid pieces called the sacrum and the illia. The sacrum, a triangular piece of bone, is flanked on either side by the two illia, which are attached to it by ligaments and connected to each other in front by a strong thick ligament forming a joint known as the *symphysis pubis*. On either side of the pelvis are two sockets, the *acetabula*, into which the ball-like ends of the thigh bones fit. These sockets form the hip joints.

The pelvis is, therefore, the connecting structure between the spine and the hips and legs, or between the top and bottom halves of the body. A solid ring of bone, it acts like a giant couple or an enormous hinge—a central axle from which the body pivots, with the legs pushing up on it and the spine pushing down. Because the pelvis is the connecting and central point, it follows that the position of the pelvis will control the position of the lumbar vertebrae above it. If the pelvis is level or, as I prefer to call it, balanced, the vertebrae above it will also be in a level or balanced position. This is the strongest and healthiest position for the spine and makes it the least vulnerable to injury. If, however, the pelvis is thrust forward, the vertebrae above it will curve out of alignment. When these lumbar vertebrae are out of alignment it makes the spine weak and vulnerable to injury by causing wedging of the disc space and potential discomfort to the facet joints. When the spine is aligned properly because the pelvis is in a

THE PELVIS: a solid, boney foundation
for the lumbar vertebrae

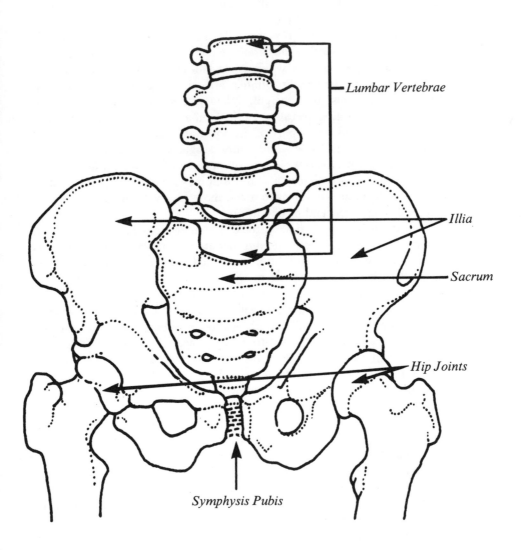

Lumbar Vertebrae

Illia

Sacrum

Hip Joints

Symphysis Pubis

BALANCED PELVIS: strongest position for the back

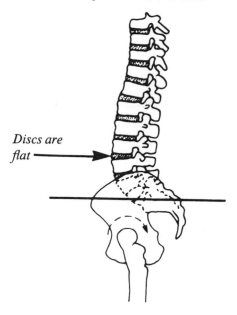

Discs are flat →

UNBALANCED PELVIS: weak position which is vulnerable to injury

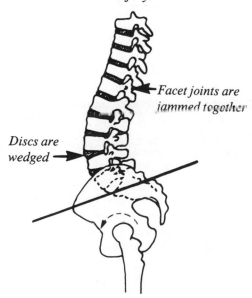

Facet joints are jammed together

Discs are wedged →

balanced position, pressure is taken off the discs, the facet joints are unloaded, and maximum space is provided for the nerve root.

Thus patients with backaches should rest in bed in the balanced pelvic position. Our physiotherapist teaches them how to rest in this position. In a later chapter I'll go into this subject at greater length.

The Other Side
of Backache

Now that I've given you a fast look at the way the bones and discs of the spine work, let's return to our friend Skinny. The ligaments, cartilage, tendons, and muscles hold up the spine, and you will recall that Skinny is hanging from a suspension bar because he has lost these means of support. The ligaments are the tough bands of tissue that connect one bone to another; the tendons connect muscles to bones; cartilage functions as a shock absorber between the bones; and the muscles are the dynamic support of the whole skeletal system.

The bones are the static, unchangeable part of the body. The muscles are the dynamic component, giving life and movement to the body. Back muscles play an important part in backache, as Margaret discovered. They are the changeable, controllable element, responding to the environment and controlled by our conscious thought processes. Composed of contractible fibers that are responsive to nervous impulses, muscles comprise 40 per cent of our body weight, a large part of the body's bulk. There are some 140 muscles attached to the spine alone and they do a prodigious amount of work.

You could compare the muscles to tiny factories that convert chemicals (food and oxygen are burned) into mechanical energy for movement. The mind, acting like a computer, controls movement, thinking and formulating messages to the muscles, which carry them out. A muscle is basically contractile tissue; that is, it functions and carries out messages by contracting or shortening and relaxing or lengthening. Muscle strength develops the more the muscle is used or worked. If it is not used as much as it should be it weakens and becomes flabby. If it is not used at all it atrophies or wastes away.

We are going to dwell on the specific muscles that are associated with and support the spine—the back muscles. This term "back muscles" can be very misleading. When we refer to back muscles we do not mean the muscles in the back but the muscles *in* and *associated with* the back. The four groups of muscles we will refer to as back muscles are synergistic, which means that they all work together and are interdependent. All four groups are, therefore, essential to the proper functioning of the back.

The erector spinae

1. These back muscles, which hold the spine erect, are not visible to the naked eye. You can feel them if you stand up and put your hands on your hips with your thumbs on the middle line of the backbone. Move the thumbs about an inch to the side; hold your hands firmly on the back while you walk on the spot and you will feel these muscles alternately contracting and relaxing while they hold the spine erect. They provide posterior support for the back and get their heaviest workout when you push or pull heavy weights, bend over, arch your back, or hold your spine very erectly.

The rectus abdominus

2. People are often surprised to learn that these abdominal muscles are very important back muscles. Two straps or bands of muscles, they run from the ribcage to the sides and front of the pelvis, providing support to the front of the spine as well as supporting the contents of the abdominal cavity.

The lateral muscles

3. These muscles lie against the side walls of the trunk. If you place your hands just above your hips you will feel them. They run in a criss-crossed fashion (like weaving they are criss-crossed for strength). Included in this group are the internal and external oblique muscles and the *quadratus lumborum,* which help control the sideways bending of the spine.

The hip muscles

There are four groups of muscles performing as one unit for each hip. They are called.

- *The hip flexors:* Located at the front of the hip, these muscles allow you to bend the leg at the hip. The most important one is called the *psoas major.* It is located at each side of the spine, deep inside the abdomen, and passes over the pelvis and hip joint to attach to the thigh. It acts like a giant sling preventing the body from falling forward.
- *The hip abductors:* Located on the side of the hip, they provide stability for the hip and allow you to keep your balance, even if you are standing on one leg.

THE BACK MUSCLES

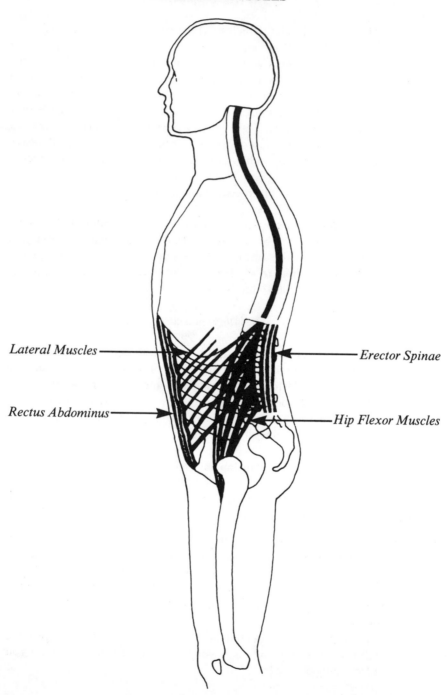

Lateral Muscles

Rectus Abdominus

Erector Spinae

Hip Flexor Muscles

THE HYDRAULIC SAC MECHANISM

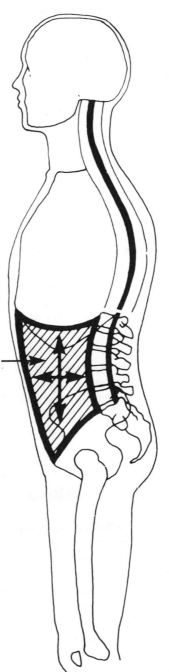

ABDOMINAL CAVITY:
an enclosed sac of fluid and air which
causes weight-bearing forces to be
distributed in all directions, providing
support for the lower back.

- *The hip adductors:* These are groin muscles that provide stability for the pelvis and enable the legs to be pulled together.
- *The hip extensors:* These are massive muscles at the back of the hip. The most prominent, the *gluteus maximus,* enables you to climb and run. The hamstring muscles, which run from the bottom of the pelvis to the back of the knee, ensure flexibility in the hip and knee joints.

So we have four sets of back muscles working together to support the spine. Imagine the pelvis floating on an axis, held down by the hip extensors and flexors and held up by the lateral, back, and abdominal muscles. The pelvic foundation on which the lower spine rests is, therefore, levelled or balanced by muscular action. If you recall that the spine is in proper working alignment when the pelvis is in the balanced position, you can readily see that the four interdependent groups of muscles must all be working properly to keep the spine balanced. If any of these muscles is weak because it's too short or too long, the spine will not be in proper alignment and there will be extra wear and tear on it, increasing the probability of backache.

Then there's a fascinating mechanism that provides extra support for the spine. It's called the hydraulic sac mechanism and is created by the co-ordinated contraction of the stomach and back muscles, diaphragm, and pelvic floor muscles. When these muscles tighten simultaneously, the abdominal cavity, which is an enclosed sac of fluid, air, and organs, gives added support to the spine. For example, when the spine is called on to lift a heavy load, the hydraulic sac helps equalize the effort so the total weight of the load is not transmitted entirely through the spine but is absorbed throughout the abdominal cavity. More on this in chapter 10.

How Your
Muscles Work

As I mentioned earlier in the chapter, muscles are basically contractile tissue; that is, they function by contracting or shortening and relaxing or lengthening. Let's look now at the difference between isotonic and isometric muscular contraction. You have probably seen those terms many times before, but do you understand what they mean? Isotonic means equal tone or tension in a muscle (ISO—equal, TONIC—tone). While the tension in a muscle remains the same, the length of the muscle changes. This type of contraction basically occurs when muscles move joints. For example, when we jump up and down or wave goodbye we are making isotonic muscular contractions.

An isometric contraction (ISO–equal, METRIC–length) means that the tension of the muscle changes but the length remains the same. This kind of contraction happens when we make a fist or hold an arm out horizontally. There is no movement at the joint, but the muscle is generating effort to maintain the position.

If you recall, during my discussion with Margaret I asked her to make a fist, hold it, and describe the feeling. She was making an isometric contraction of the muscle and discovered that it first began to tremble and then became uncomfortable after several seconds. Static muscular effort cannot be continued for very long because the blood supply, which provides energy or fuel to the muscle, is squeezed out. This causes waste materials to build up in the muscle, which finally produce discomfort.

In an isotonic contraction the muscles move, pushing the blood through the stretched muscle and the waste materials are flushed out. Isotonic contractions of the back muscles cause back movement of the kind needed by a dancer. Isometric contractions of the back muscles create the trunk stability and strength needed by a weight lifter.

The strength of a muscle depends on its bulk or size–and its length. This relationship is shown in the accompanying diagram of the Blix curve,

BLIX CURVE: *muscle strength is dependent on the length of muscles, strongest in the middle position, weakest when too long or too short*

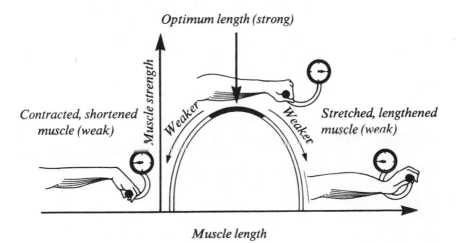

Muscle length

which simply illustrates that a muscle is *strongest* at its *optimum length*. If the muscle is stretched past or becomes shorter than its optimum length, it becomes weaker. If you would like to examine this effect try the "wrist test." Hold your wrist straight and make a fist. Notice the strength and stability of the wrist and how easily a fist is made when the wrist is held in the optimum position of length. Bend the wrist back and see how difficult it is to make a fist when the muscles are shortened and no longer in the optimum position. The same results will take place if you bend the wrist forward, thereby stretching the muscles out of the optimum position. Notice too, how strong the impulse is to put the wrist back into the position where it will be stronger and more stable.

Now let's see what happens when a muscle is stretched excessively for long periods of time. For example, the abdominal muscles (remember that they, too, are back muscles) become stretched and weaker during pregnancy. People who carry a lot of extra poundage on their bellies also stretch the abdominal muscles. If these muscles have become stretched and incapable of providing the necessary support to the spine, the other sets of back muscles are forced to take on extra work to compensate for them. Thus the other muscles become fatigued, and may become strained and finally react with pain and spasm. In the majority of backache cases it's weakness in one or more sets of back muscles that is the primary cause of the problem.

A muscle becomes shorter and weaker when it is contracted for long periods without accompanying stretching movements. Let's return to Margaret's backache as an example. An injured muscle will contract when it goes into spasm and even after the pain subsides the muscle will tend to remain shortened and weak. I don't think many people realize that unless they exercise to stretch the injured muscle back to its optimum working length the back will be even more vulnerable than before the first attack. Why? Before the attack, the back muscles were the proper working length—after the injury, the spasmed muscles will be shorter and place more strain on the other sets of muscles. A sudden trauma or injury to the back resulting in an immediate painful effect is often the underlying cause of the first episode of back pain. But unless reconditioning steps are taken after the pain has subsided, the weakened back is susceptible to repeated or chronic trauma. In a sedentary society we become prone to back trauma. Our muscles, deprived of sustained exercise, become stretched and flabby. No longer capable of vigorous activity, the muscles will be strained and fatigued by an unusual exertion. As Margaret was beginning to learn from our short anatomy course, if an underlying cause of backache is weak back muscles, the only hope for total recovery lies in physical reconditioning. That's why a doctor can't prevent future backaches unless the patient determines to do a share of the work. Fortunately, the National Back Fitness Test in this book will quickly point out which of your back muscles need reconditioning. And it doesn't take much effort or much time. Just five to ten minutes of simple exercises each day will keep your back in good shape for the rest of your life. You'll be able to say, "Goodbye, backache!" and mean it.

5

How to Relieve a Backache

When patients come to me with backache there is only one thing they want—relief from the pain. I don't blame them. Pain is one of the worst human afflictions, robbing people of the will to accomplish anything in life. For chronic sufferers, it is such a debilitating problem that it becomes almost a disease in itself, and the main purpose of early treatment is to alleviate it. Pain, as we have seen, can lead to muscle spasm and spasm, in a vicious cycle, can lead to more pain. The earlier the cycle is interrupted the faster the back will heal.

Pain is a highly subjective phenomenon, interpreted differently in each patient according to the way each has been trained by culture and education to accept it. It's well known that professional athletes often continue to play despite injuries that would sideline the rest of us. They've learned to push their bodies to the limits of performance and tolerate pain, which is anesthetized by the excitement of the moment. But no matter where the patient's attitudes come from, fear and uncertainty will make it more difficult to endure pain. Positive suggestions can work wonders and even the promise of relief can help a great deal. I'm sure most of you have had the experience of going to the doctor in pain and feeling it decrease, sometimes even vanish, while you're still sitting in the waiting room. You're sure the doctor will think you a complete fool. But the doctor realizes that because you knew help was at hand you relaxed and the pain became more bearable. During a hockey game while I was in medical school a puck smashed into my face, fracturing my cheekbone. I felt panicky during the ride to the emergency department. My right eye was so swollen I couldn't see out of it and I wondered if I'd lose the eye. As soon as I was in the emergency room with a doctor the panic left me. It's called transference—the problem was the doctor's now, not mine.

There are three types of pain, each with different characters and meanings, involved in backache. The first is *acute pain,* which is sharp, intense, immediate, and unexpected—for example, the kind you feel if you hit your thumb with a hammer. With acute pain there will be an inability to rest comfortably and any movement of the affected part of the back increases pain, sometimes to the point where medication is required. The second type, *chronic pain,* is constant, dull, and unremitting, although the mind can be diverted from it by excitement. *Mild pain,* the third type, might be better classified as discomfort and stiffness. It is often noticed upon rising in the morning and the normal daily activities usually alleviate it. This type of discomfort is a gentle reminder that all is not well with the back.

A patient's normal response to pain is to withdraw from activity; that is, to avoid any stimulus that aggravates it. There is also a tendency to immobilize the affected part. But most people don't respond in a normal way to *back* pain. Because it's inconvenient to immobilize the back they plod on in their usual fashion, often ending up with an acute attack of backache that totally incapacitates them.

Frightened by this experience, the patient, in an attempt to forestall another attack of acute back pain, will often respond to chronic back pain in the wrong way: avoidance of stimulus and exercise. That response, while valid for acute pain, may only serve to increase chronic pain. Pain then becomes the focus of the patient's life.

Because I want the pain cycle broken quickly, I suggest to my patients that they learn to rest their backs in the way that will best speed up the healing process. Although I know they won't be able to grasp the whole picture, especially when they're concentrating on the pain, I still offer a short anatomy course on the back so there is some understanding of the validity of my suggestion. I also want them to understand that the absence of pain does not mean the back is cured. I emphasize this to them because it is absolutely necessary that they return for fitness testing and instruction in back exercise if they are needed. But the last thing I want them to do during an acute attack of back pain is any form of exercise or anything at all that will aggravate it. My main goal at the beginning of treatment is to provide relief from pain.

How to Rest
in Bed

In the last chapter I explained why the balanced pelvis was the position of strength and health for the back. It is also the position that encourages healing for a painful back.

GOOD BED-REST POSITIONS:
the pelvis is balanced

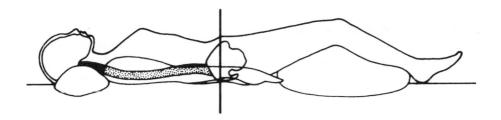

The back rest: knees bent and comfortably supported by a pillow

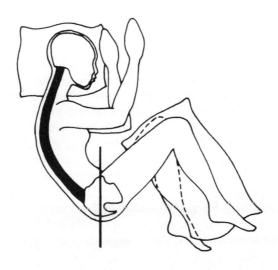

The foetal position: pillow between the knees to prevent twisting of the spine

For bed rest, this position can be accomplished very simply. The patient should lie on the back with the head resting comfortably on a pillow and with the lower legs supported by pillows behind the knees to ensure that the pelvis is flat against the bed or in the balanced position. The mattress should be firm enough that the body does not sag. If the mattress is too soft, an inexpensive plywood bedboard should be placed under it.

Many patients find that the floor is even more comfortable than bed. The patient lies on the floor, head and buttocks supported by pillows with the legs up on the bed. I know patients who often sleep in this position all night when they have an attack of backache. It's also a good defensive position to take whenever you feel a back twinge coming on. The only difference is that you can switch to a chair instead of a bed. Lie on the floor, head and buttocks supported by pillows and legs resting on a chair, with the trunk of the body moved as far under the chair as possible. You can watch TV at night in this position after a strenuous day and unload and relax your fatigued spine. It feels so good that you may find yourself becoming addicted to it.

The foetal position is another way to relax the spine while resting in bed. Roll over to one side with the hips and knees bent toward the chest and the head on a pillow. Place another pillow between the knees; this one is very important beause it supports the upper leg so that circulation in the lower leg will not be obstructed.

It doesn't matter which of the two positions you adopt while resting in bed, but it is important that the position be changed frequently. It's necessary and natural for the body to move. Recent sleep studies have shown that although we are largely unaware of movement, our bodies twist and turn all night. These movements ensure proper blood circulation and also prevent the joints and muscles from becoming stiff. If you are going to be lying in bed with a backache the last thing you want is *more* stiffness. Changing your positions will help prevent discomfort and keep the blood circulating properly.

Here's one last tip for people suffering from acute spasm. It will be easier to get out of bed if you roll onto your side and push your trunk up with both your arms. Your legs can easily slide over the edge of the bed to the floor.

Home Remedies

There is only one main rule to remember when applying home remedies: if it makes you feel better, use it; if it makes you feel worse, discontinue it.

Heat

Heat has been used as a remedy for pain by every race throughout the centuries. Even animals seem to know that heat will relieve aches and pains—watch an old rheumatic dog and see how it searches out the sunniest part of the yard to warm its bones. Heat improves the blood supply to the muscle so that the toxic wastes can be flushed out. One of the great assets of heat therapy is its convenience; use whatever is handy in the house—a hot water bottle, heating pad, hot wet towels, or take a warm bath or shower. The more expensive methods of applying heat are not much more valuable than the cheaper methods, so there's no need to rush off and buy the newest heat appliance.

For some people wet heat is the most effective, for others dry heat works best. Whatever method you prefer is fine but make sure that you employ it long enough for it to take proper effect—15 to 20 minutes should do. Remember that no matter how comfortable you become, your back should not be held in one position for too long—this could lead to stiffness and pain when you move and you could re-establish the old cycle of muscle spasm, pain, and spasm.

Heat therapy should be applied several times a day but *please be careful*! Don't become so comfortable you doze off and burn yourself. As a precaution I advise patients, especially those living alone, to set an alarm clock to ring 15 minutes after the heat is applied. Remember also that it is not necessary for the heat to be so intense that you're uncomfortable. Some people think the hotter the better. It's not true—gentle heat is just as beneficial.

Many people find soaking in a hot tub very soothing but the good effects are countered for some by the pain caused by getting in or out. Again, it's up to you. If it feels good and you have no problem getting in or out then go ahead and do it. Hot showers are also beneficial and the pounding water directed on your back can help the circulation.

Cold

When there has been significant trauma to the back and the blood vessels have been torn with resulting bruises caused by the ruptured veins and arteries, cold packs are the preferred method of treatment. While heat expands the blood vessels, cold does just the opposite—it helps constrict the blood vessels and stop the bleeding. It also helps relieve the pain by anesthetizing the area. It should be applied intermittently for 24 to 48 hours after the injury, then, heat should be the method of treatment. In prescribing cold therapy, the doctor faces a real problem because there is no way to determine whether the blood vessels in the back have been torn. The doctor will, therefore, have to make a judgement based on experience. Generally, I prefer to use heat therapy—it's an effective treatment for muscle spasm and cold packs can often be very uncomfortable. If you have discovered that the application of cold at the beginning of treatment is beneficial to your back, here's a tip to eliminate some of the discomfort from a wet, messy bed. Put ice cubes in a plastic bag, seal the bag and wrap it in a damp towel before placing the "ice pack" on the painful area.

As I've said, heat is preferred by most people, who find it more comfortable, but neither method can harm you. Remember to gently stretch the spasmodic muscles after an application of either heat or cold.

Counter-irritants

If you find the application of heat or cold insufficient for total relief from pain, a counter-irritant may help. They work by confusing the nerve endings, providing distraction from the original pain. They also cause a nervous reflex that leads to dilation of the blood vessels, an effect somewhat similar to the application of heat. I advocate the use of milder rubs gently massaged into the back. There's no need to use anything that is intensely irritating or even uncomfortable.

Massage

A gentle massage not only helps loosen up a muscle spasm, it also increases the blood supply to the muscles. The psychological benefits are almost as important as the physiological ones. It feels marvellous to be given a simple, light stroking massage by someone you like in a comfortably warm room. Stroking the body has a soothing effect, as any mother of a small child instinctively knows. The human contact shows support, concern, and sympathy, which help to relax the entire body. Light massage can be given as often as needed for ten minutes at a time, and should be gentle and painless.

Manipulation

There is no doubt that under many conditions manipulation can be useful in the treatment of back pain. Manipulation consists of putting a joint through a range of movements. When there has been subluxation of a joint or acute muscle spasm, manipulation can be valuable. More and more physicians now employ it in treating back pain and it is the main method of treatment used by chiropractors and osteopaths. The difference between chiropractors and the doctors who use manipulation lies in philosophy rather than application. Chiropractors believe that disease can be caused by interference or blockage of the nervous impulses coming out from the spine to the body's organs and extremities. They believe that manipulation or adjustment of the spine will restore health to the affected part of the body. Doctors consider manipulation solely a treatment that breaks down joint adhesions and relieves muscle spasms. I think the main point to keep in mind about manipulation is that an accurate diagnosis of the back problem must be made before this kind of treatment is given. Manipulation, as should be evident to anyone with common sense, does not cure pathological conditions such as cancer or tuberculosis.

The chiropractor has one main method of treatment compared to the many used by medical doctors. Unless a diagnosis of the back problem has been made, the chiropractic treatment, while providing some measure of temporary relief, may mask a serious condition that needs a more specific type of therapy. Manipulation can be dangerous when certain diseases are causing the problem. For example, when backache is the result of an acute disc herniation, it may make matters worse for the patient if manipulation increases pressure on the nerve root that is being irritated by the extruding nucleus pulposis. Take, for another example, a patient with osteoporosis, a disease affecting the density of the spinal bones. Too much pressure on the spine during a manipulation treatment can fracture the thinning vertebrae. You can understand from these examples why it is so important to have an accurate diagnosis made before this kind of treatment. However, there are cases I have witnessed where manipulation has worked wonders.

One day a doctor who specialized in manipulation was visiting the Back Care Centre. That morning a patient crawled into my office, terribly bent over with back pain. A few days before he had been involved in a lifting accident at the brick company where he worked. He had been carried home in such agony from muscle spasm that his family doctor had given him injections of Demerol for the intense pain. I examined the patient and then suggested to my colleague that he might be a good test subject for manipulation. I have to admit that at that time I was fairly skeptical and I guess it showed. My friend cheerfully agreed and led my patient off to the table where he examined his back. As the patient was laid face down and my friend began to manipulate his spine, I heard a terrific crack followed by a muffled shout. Nervously, I rushed to help the man down from the table. "Praise God," he shouted as he stood up and literally began to skip up and down, "Praise God, the pain's completely gone!" During a break with the doctor later that morning, I'm afraid I had to wash down a little humble pie with my coffee.

This story emphasizes the problem a doctor faces when it comes to advising manipulation therapy—it's very hard to know *which* patient will benefit from it. Let me just say that if you are going for manipulation therapy your back pain should be improving after three to six treatments. If it isn't or if it's getting worse, manipulation obviously isn't working for you and the diagnosis should be reconsidered.

Analgesics

One of the most useful pain-killers for backache is aspirin. In cases associated with injury or disease where there is inflammation it can often produce dramatic results because of its anti-inflammatory effect. Taken at night before you go to sleep it can also help reduce stiffness and pain on awakening. For severe back pain such pure analgesics as codeine are added to the aspirin for greater potency. The newer anti-inflammatory drugs— phenobutalzone, for example—are considered effective for such back diseases as ankylosing spondylitis, which is caused by inflammation. Your doctor will be able to advise you which analgesic will work best.

Tranquillizers

I recommend tranquillizers to some of my patients who will be lying in bed for fairly long periods. They reduce emotional tension, which in turn helps to relax muscle spasm. If patients are worried that they will become habit-forming, I quickly reassure them that the minute they begin to feel better they can discontinue the tranquillizers. The same goes for analgesics—as soon as they are no longer necessary for a good night's sleep, cut them off.

There is one reason and one reason only for taking medications and applying home remedies for a backache: they make you feel better while you are getting better. None of the remedies listed in this chapter will cure a backache—only rest and time will make the pain go away. You should keep in mind that short-term measures for pain relief are fine as long as they don't become substitutes for preventive long-term action.

As a case in point, let's return to my patient Margaret. A week after I had sent her home to rest in bed she came back for her appointment. She was entirely free of backache and, as could be expected, it was a different woman I now met in my office. Enthusiastic and full of energy, she was off all pain medication and eager to return to work. I examined her back and found that the muscle spasm was greatly reduced and her range of movement much improved.

"Even though you feel terrific you're not quite your old self," I told her. "The acute phase of back pain is over but you must exercise caution for a few weeks when it comes to any demands you make on your back. I want you to come and see me again in a month. Your back should be fully healed by then and you can try our back fitness tests. I suspect you have weak back muscles and, if so, we'll show you what exercises you can do to improve the muscles and avoid future bouts of backache."

"Okay, I'll be back," Margaret said. "While I was at home an old friend came to see me. He's been suffering from back pain for the past ten years. I can tell you, I was so depressed by his story that I resolved to do anything I could to prevent that happening to me. That poor guy's been in and out of surgery and he's still in pain. And he's only a few years older than me. There's no way I want to end up in that condition. I'll see you in a month, doctor."

The following chapter explains the National Back Fitness Test. Why don't you try it and see how your back measures up?

6

The National Back Fitness Test

The National Back Fitness Test consists of four simple tests that help you determine if your back is strong and healthy or weak and unfit. The results may reassure you that you have little to worry about, but more likely, given the way we live now, they will warn you that your back is vulnerable to injury and strain. The tests look so easy it's hard to believe so many people perform them so poorly. If you have suffered back injuries be prepared to wash out, unless you have undertaken a specific reconditioning program.

These tests are not the same ones a doctor gives you when he's examining your back for disease. The doctor, who is looking for range of movement, muscle strength, and reflex sensations, usually conducts tests while the back is painful. They are of little use in determining if it is strong or weak. The back fitness tests, on the other hand, are performed while the back is asymptomatic or pain-free and are far more valuable in measuring back function. They will demonstrate how much muscle weakness and joint stiffness are contributing to your back problem—or, if you don't have one yet, indicate that chances are you will.

In the past, people who have suffered from backache have not been given guidelines telling them just what shape their backs are in. All anyone with a back problem could do was hope that nothing would go wrong. But the back fitness tests will show you just what shape your back is in so you can determine the level of stress it can withstand.

Perhaps you've never had a backache or only the occasional twinge. Why should you try the tests? Have you thought lately about the ravages of our sedentary style of living? Remember that the first muscles to deteriorate when we are unfit are the stomach and back muscles. If these muscles are weak, your back is probably not working as well as it should be. The back is a very delicate, balanced, and complex mechanism—it is only as strong as its weakest link.

The tests also show whether you have lost touch with your fitness level. Are you in as good shape as you used to be? You expect to test and tune up your car from time to time. How about your body? Try the tests and see if your back is working as well as it was a few years ago. What's more the tests are standardized and offer a comparative tool of measurement—you can find out how your back compares with those of people around you.

Once again, the tests look easy but they are actually quite difficult when done properly and with attention to detail. In fact, only about one out of ten people can perform all four tests at grade 1, the excellent level. Remember also that these four tests are *not* exercises. If you don't do well on them, read on and learn what back exercises you need and how to pace the reconditioning process. Note: these tests are appropriate only if your back is pain-free. They should not be tried if you are experiencing back pain.

The National
Back Fitness Test

Test A —
The Sit-up

The major purpose of Test A is to determine the flexibility of the back. Its minor purpose is to determine the strength of the stomach muscles.

Position

1. Lie on your back on the floor.
2. Bend your knees to a 45 degree angle, placing your feet flat on the floor.
3. Place your hands behind your neck.

Procedure

1. Slowly and smoothly try to sit up without raising your feet off the floor.
   If you are unable to sit up without your feet coming off the floor:
2. Place your arms across your chest and try to sit up again.
   If still unable to sit up:
3. Put your arms out straight and try once more to sit up.

Caution

1. Do not jerk yourself up or crank your head up with your arms. This can aggravate a neck problem. For a valid test the effort must be made slowly and smoothly.
2. Do not tuck your feet under something or have someone hold them down. This invalidates the test. It makes it easier to perform because it activates the leg muscles, which pull the back to a sitting position. Pulling yourself up in this way can also harm a weak back.

Figure 1 shows the four performance levels for Test A and the scores assigned to each.

FIGURE 1

SCORE	PERFORMANCE	BACK FITNESS
1	Able to sit up with knees bent and hands behind the neck.	Excellent: adequate spinal flexibility and stomach strength.
2	Able to sit up with knees bent and arms folded across the chest.	Good: need to improve stomach muscle strength.

| 3 | Able to sit up with knees bent and arms held out straight. | Fair: need to improve spinal flexibility and stomach strength. |

| 4 | Unable to sit up with the knees bent. | Poor: need a great deal of improvement in both strength and flexibility. |

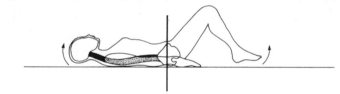

Interpretation

Many people are distressed when they fail such a simple test. This is particularly true of athletic types who appear quite muscular. What they have forgotten is that flexibility or suppleness of the back is just as important for fitness as strong stomach muscles. People who do quite poorly on Test A often include:

- Older people whose backs have naturally stiffened.
- Muscular individuals who have not maintained suppleness and flexibility. They often feel that they fail Test A because their upper body weight causes their feet to lift up off the ground. However, individuals with good flexibility have an ability to change their centre of gravity, allowing them to sit up despite upper body bulk.
- Individuals who have suffered back problems that have left their backs stiff.

- Individuals with pot bellies, indicating poor abdominal muscle tone and strength.
- In general, women perform this test at a higher level than men because they have better flexibility.

Test B —
Double Straight
Leg Raise

Test B determines the strength of the abdominal or stomach muscles.

Position

1. Lie on your back on the floor with your legs straight out in front of you.
2. Place your hands between the hollow of your back and the floor.

Procedure

1. Eliminate the hollow between your back and the floor by tightening your stomach muscles and forcing your back tightly against your hands on the floor. There should be no space. Keep your back held tightly against the floor.
2. Firmly hold this position and simultaneously raise both feet ten inches off the floor.
3. Hold the feet up for ten counts keeping the back tightly pressed against the floor.

Caution

If your lower back begins to curve after raising your legs or if back pain is felt, do not continue. Back strain may result from lifting the legs when the back is not held in the flat balanced pelvic position. Remember that this is a test and not an exercise. Once you have determined your score, stop the testing. This test can be harmful if it is performed continuously while the back is weak.

Figure 2 shows the four performance levels for Test B and the scores assigned to each.

FIGURE 2

SCORE	PERFORMANCE	BACK FITNESS
1	Able to keep the back flat while raising the legs for ten seconds.	Excellent: can demonstrate balanced pelvic position and hold it under extreme stress.

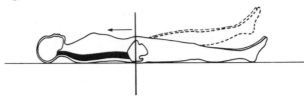

2	Able to raise the legs for several seconds, but the back curves part way through the test.	Good: can demonstrate balanced pelvic position, but need more stomach muscle strength and training to hold good posture under extreme stress.

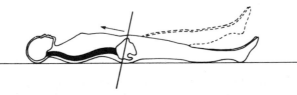

3	Able to lift the legs, but the back curves as soon as the legs are raised.	Fair: need training in balanced pelvic position and increased stomach muscle strength.

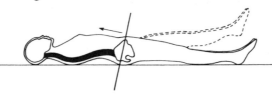

4	Unable to lift both legs.	Poor: need extensive training in balanced pelvic position and increased stomach muscle strength.

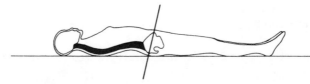

Pitfalls

Curling the head off the floor makes the test easier. Your body, including your head, should be held straight out to make the test valid. Lifting the legs too high also makes the test easier and invalidates it. It is most important to keep the hollow of the back flat against the floor because this determines the grade. Most people tend to concentrate, instead, on the effort of raising the legs.

Interpretation

Everyone should aim for Grade 1 on this test. Age is no barrier to good performance provided the stomach muscles are strong enough. This test shows whether the stomach muscles can hold the balanced pelvic position under stressful conditions, such as when you are playing sports or lifting heavy objects. It also shows whether you have the ability to flatten the back and eliminate the hollow in the lower back when your legs are held straight out. If you can't eliminate the hollow, bend your knees and try again. If you can get rid of the hollow when your knees are bent, it indicates that you have short hip flexors and you will do poorly on Test D.

Test C —
Lateral Trunk Lift

Test C determines the strength of the lateral muscles of the trunk and legs.

Position

1. You will need someone to assist you in this test. Lie on your right side with your legs straight out and look straight ahead.
2. Fold your arms across your chest.
3. Have your assistant firmly hold your feet down by the ankles so that they do not rise off the floor during the test.

Procedure

1. Slowly and smoothly raise your shoulders and upper body off the floor.
2. Raise your shoulders up as far as possible and hold for ten counts.
3. Return to the starting position.
4. Repeat, testing the other side of your body.

Caution

If there is pain or discomfort stop the test.

Figure 3 shows the four performance levels for Test C and the scores assigned to each.

FIGURE 3

SCORE	PERFORMANCE	BACK FITNESS
1	Able to raise the upper body completely and hold for ten counts.	Excellent: adequate lateral trunk muscles.

2	Able to raise the upper body up with difficulty and cannot hold for ten counts.	Good: need to improve lateral trunk muscles.

3	Able to raise the upper body a few inches and unable to hold.	Fair: need improvement in lateral trunk muscles.

4	Unable to raise the body off the floor.	Poor: need much improvement in lateral trunk muscles.

Pitfalls

Do not jerk or jump the body up; this invalidates the test. So does pushing up from the elbow. Your body must be perfectly straight while lying on your side. Many people substitute other muscle groups by allowing the body to drift forward or backward while they are lifting the upper body.

Interpretation

This test determines the strength of the lateral trunk and leg muscles, which are critical for upright posture. When you are lying on your right side, you are testing the muscles in your left side and vice versa. People who experience fatigue or discomfort in the lower back after jogging, long walks, or forward bending (while sweeping or raking, for example), usually do poorly on this test. It is important to compare the performance on the right and left sides. A poor performance on just one side of the body usually correlates with past injury to the side being tested.

Test D — The Hip Flexors

This test determines the length of the hip flexors (the psoas muscles), which prevent you from falling forward while standing.

Position

1. Wearing loose clothing, lie on the floor with your legs straight out in front of you.

Procedure

1. Bend your right leg, bringing it toward the chest.
2. Grasp the knee and complete the movement by bringing your leg tightly against the chest.
3. Hold your knee to your chest and determine the position of the other leg. Is the entire leg lying flat against the floor? Is the leg partially or completely raised off the floor?
4. Place both legs straight out on the floor and repeat the test by bringing the left leg up against the chest. Now determine the position of the right leg.

Figure 4 shows the four performance levels for Test D and the scores assigned to each.

FIGURE 4

SCORE	PERFORMANCE	BACK FITNESS
1	Able to bring your knee completely to chest and keep the other leg flat on the floor.	Excellent: hip flexors are the proper length.

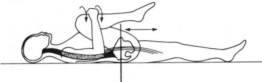

| 2 | Able to bring your knee to your chest but the other leg lifts slightly off the floor. | Good: need to slightly stretch hip flexors. |

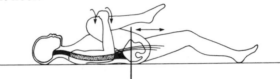

| 3 | Leg lifts completely off the floor when your knee is pulled to your chest. | Fair: need much improvement in hip flexors length. |

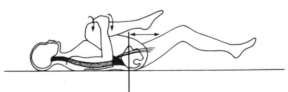

| 4 | Leg flies up into the air when your knee is held against your chest. | Poor: inadequate length of hip flexors — they need a great deal of stretching. |

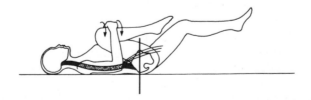

Pitfalls

The head must remain on the floor and the knee must be held snugly to the chest. The critical upward movement of the leg lying on the floor occurs during the last part of the test.

Interpretation

We know that shortness of muscles means weakness. Short hip flexors indicate a vulnerability to back injury because these are the critical anti-gravity muscles used for upright posture, lifting, and bending. Bilateral shortening, or shortening on both sides, usually occurs in athletic individuals. It often causes the "athletic bum", the increased lower back hollow of many athletes and dancers. Normally this condition does not cause backache in athletes, but if the abdominal muscles become weak later in life or a pot belly forms, there will be a tendency to back problems. Unilateral or one-sided shortening often correlates with a serious injury to that side and is associated with a pain down that leg. It is associated as well with a lateral muscle weakness on that side.

Total Back
Fitness Score

Use the scoring chart below to calculate total back fitness score. Circle your grade for each test.

		Excellent	*Good*	*Fair*	*Poor*
Test A					
Sit-up		1	2	3	4
Test B					
Leg Raise		1	2	3	4
Test C	R	½	1	1-½	2
Lateral Trunk Lift	L	½	1	1-½	2
Test D	L	½	1	1-½	2
Hip Flexors	R	½	1	1-½	2
TOTAL					

NOTE: If you are over 45, subtract 2 to reach your total score.

A score of 4 or 5 means your back is in excellent shape.
A score of 6 to 9 means your back is in average shape.
A score of 10 to 13 means your back is in fair shape.
A score of 14 to 16 means your back is in poor shape.

These tests show how well your back is functioning. If your performance was less than excellent, you've got some work to do to prevent back problems. The next chapter shows you which exercises will help your particular back weaknesses.

7

How to Strengthen Your Weak Back

Congratulations if you scored well on the National Back Fitness Test. Chances are, though, that you didn't. Take comfort; you are not alone— nine out of ten people who try it discover their backs are not in good shape. Our sedentary living habits show up on the test in three ways: stretched abdominal muscles, weak lateral trunk muscles, and shortened hip flexors.

In an earlier chapter I explained that each of the body's muscles has an optimum working length. Stretched or contracted for a long time, the muscle weakens and becomes prone to injury and spasm. Get those muscles into working shape and you will eliminate the potential for chronic backache, which could eventually turn into a more serious and disabling ailment. But not to worry—just a few minutes of simple exercise each day will work wonders.

Why do exercises work? Because it's nature's way. Our backs are so important for bodily health and function that nature has structured their strong working muscles to compensate for all sorts of stresses. If you have arthritis of the spine, degenerating discs, or any other back disease that does not need corrective surgery, a regimen of appropriate exercise will enable you to live a pain-free, active life. You'll forget you ever had a back problem.

The purpose of the reconditioning exercise program presented in this chapter is to restore your back muscles to their proper length. The program provides two types of exercises: *power-strength,* which will tighten up and shorten the stretched abdominal and lateral trunk muscles, and *stretch-relaxation,* which will lengthen the contracted hip flexors.

Because people vary in their capabilities, the program has been devised to accommodate varying fitness levels depending on age, sex, and previous conditioning. Since we first developed the National Back Fitness Test, we have learned what to predict for certain types of people:

1. Those over the age of 45 likely have begun to lose flexibility. It's a natural aging process—the back becomes stiffer with each advancing year. They'll probably need stretch-relaxation exercises to loosen up those muscles before they can get maximum benefit from the power-strength exercises.

2. Our tests show that while women generally are more flexible than men, they are not as strong and usually need power-strength exercises.

3. Men, to be sure, are stronger but they are much less supple than women and usually need stretch-relaxation exercises that will increase their flexibility.

4. We've also found that while athletic individuals have a better muscle base, certain types of sports predispose them to short, contracted back muscles. They often need compensating stretch-relaxation exercises.

5. Finally, those who have suffered from back problems and whose backs have healed with short, contracted muscles usually need both power-strength and strength-relaxation exercises.

How about you? Where do you fit in these categories?

Getting Started

As we are all aware, the biggest roadblock to an exercise program is getting started. We all have a million excuses and over the years in my Back Care Centre I'm sure I've heard every one of them. "I just don't have the time," is one of the most common, closely followed by "I'm too tired," or "I'll be late for work if I take the time in the morning." Construction and factory workers are the hardest to convince. "My job keeps me fit," they tell me, their eyes focussed on bulging biceps while they studiously ignore their flabby stomachs. Nevertheless, they have ended up in my care and I'm sometimes obliged to tactfully point this out to them. Other familiar reasons are, "I have arthritis so I can't exercise," "I'm too old," and "exercises are boring."

The last excuse is true—exercises *are* boring but, then, so is lying in bed with a backache. It's too bad our backs can't be completely fixed up with pills, operations, heat therapy, or the newest gadget on the market. It's too bad we can't bank back fitness for life. It's also too bad there is no other remedy for muscular deficiency but exercise. There is, however some good news—even though we can't control aging, accidents, heredity factors, and some illnesses, we can at least control muscular weakness. And if we improve our back fitness level we can avoid some of the problems we can't control. We can keep our backs flexible and supple even though we are growing older; we can ward off and control back diseases; we can improve the reserve capacity of our backs so that there is a built-in safety valve to counteract that fall or slip on the factory floor, that excessively heavy load we are obliged to carry, that suddenly overstretched muscle in the gymnasium.

The first step to ovecoming inertia is to *realize* that if you scored less than excellent on the back fitness test, your back needs remedial exercises. The second step is to *decide* you want a healthy pain-free back. The third step is to *commit* yourself to the five to ten minutes of exercise required each day.

There are, after all, a lot of advantages. You'll be amazed at the difference in your body after a very short period: your stomach will flatten and you'll look younger and sexier. Your back will feel so good that your whole approach to life will change—you'll have more confidence and a lot more energy and zest. You don't need special clothes or equipment and the exercises can be done in privacy (you can do them on your office floor if you want). Best of all, there's no strain, no pain, and they only take a few minutes a day. Why don't you make the commitment? Say to yourself, "I need it, I'll give it a try."

- Commit yourself to exercise for five to ten minutes daily.
- Commit yourself to exercise for at least two weeks.
- Commit yourself to exercise in the same place every day, on a firm, carpeted surface, wearing loose clothing, and with an empty stomach.
- Commit yourself to mark in the charts the number of times you did each exercise.
- Finally, commit yourself to retest your back fitness weekly and mark it on the chart.

Here goes! You are going to be surprised at the difference you will feel in only one short week. Because the exercises look so easy and are so simple to perform many people think they can't possibly make much difference. But I believe they're going to change your life.

Learning
the Pelvic Tilt

It is *essential* that you learn the balanced pelvic position or, as many call it, the pelvic tilt, before you begin the reconditioning exercises. Here's why: you can't hurt your back when you are in this position. As you have already learned, your back is at its strongest when it is in the balanced pelvic position because it places the spine in a straighter, more neutral posture. Remember the wrist test? The more curved the spine is, the more loaded the joints of the spine, and the more vulnerable it is to injury. The straighter the spine, the better it can absorb everyday stresses and strains.

Although the spine should be held in the balanced pelvic position 24 hours a day, this posture is impossible for people with weak back muscles. The muscles are not strong enough to maintain the pelvis in the proper position. That's why I don't pester patients to change their poor postural habits even though I know that bad posture is an expression of a weak back. Unless you are physically capable of holding your spine straight, no amount of nagging about bad posture is going to help. But once you have strengthened your weak back muscles, the principles of good posture can and should be applied. It's a mental as well as a physical training process. If you've ever seen dancers or models gliding across a stage, you've seen people who have been trained to hold themselves beautifully. If they can learn to stand and move correctly, so can you. I'll have a lot more to say about posture in a later chapter. Meanwhile, let's take the first step toward our goal—let's learn the pelvic tilt, the basic posture held during the back reconditioning exercises.

You can achieve the pelvic tilt in two ways:

1. Body position: by bending the hips and knees, whether the position is lying, standing, or sitting.
2. Muscular control: by training the stomach muscles to tilt the pelvis up and back, which indirectly straightens the spine.

Feeling
the Pelvic Tilt

Because so many of my patients seem to have some difficulty learning this simple position, I'm going to show you three different ways it can be achieved by body positions. Try them! I want you to *feel* the position as you learn it.

FEELING THE PELVIC TILT WHILE STANDING

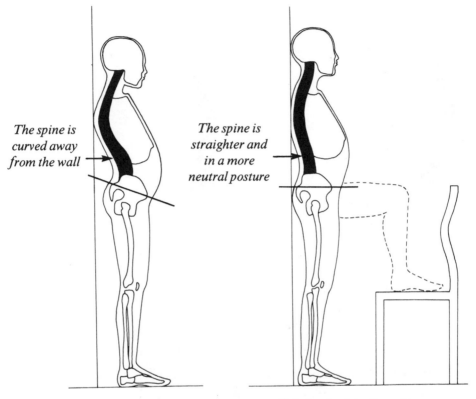

The spine is curved away from the wall →

The spine is straighter and in a more neutral posture →

Unbalanced pelvic position

Balanced pelvic tilt position

Standing procedure

1. Stand with your back and buttocks against a wall.
2. Place your hands between the hollow of your back and the wall.
3. Place one foot on a chair seat in front of you.
4. Note that your pelvis is tilted up and your back is straighter and closer to the wall than it was when both feet were on the ground. YOU ARE NOW IN THE PELVIC TILT POSITION.
5. Tighten your stomach muscles to keep your back in this position.
6. Hold this balanced pelvic position as you lower your leg to the floor.
7. Walk around the room holding this position.

FEELING THE PELVIC TILT WHILE SITTING

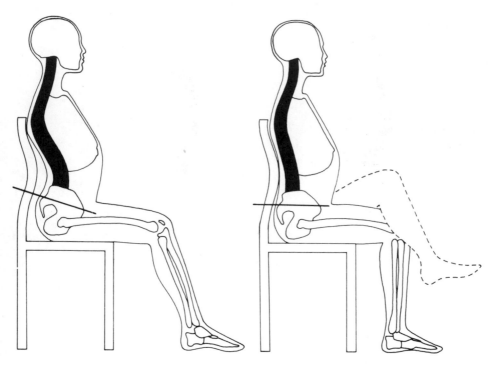

Unbalanced pelvic position   *Balanced pelvic tilt position*

Sitting procedure

1. Sit in a straight-backed chair.
2. Place your seat slightly away from the back of the chair.
3. Place your hand between the hollow of your back and the chair.
4. Cross one leg over the other and feel your pelvis push into your hands and the back of the chair. YOU ARE NOW IN THE PELVIC TILT POSITION.
5. Uncross your leg and feel your pelvis pull away from the back of the chair and your back begin to arch.

FEELING THE PELVIC TILT WHILE LYING DOWN

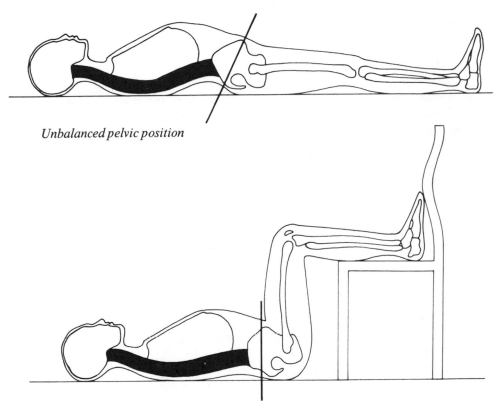

Unbalanced pelvic position

Balanced pelvic tilt position

Lying down
procedure

1. Lie on the floor with your legs straight out in front of you.
2. Place your hand between the floor and the hollow of your back.
3. Bend your knees and feel the lower back press toward the floor.
4. Now place your legs up on a chair seat and feel the back complete-ly flatten into your hands and the floor. YOU ARE NOW IN THE PELVIC TILT POSITION.

Now that you have learned what the pelvic tilt feels like we can proceed to the warm-up exercises that should be done each day at the start of the Reconditioning Exercise Program.

The following exercise is *not* supposed to tighten the back muscles and you shouldn't feel them contracting. It is not supposed to be a difficult exercise, but a deliberate rocking movement which will unload your spine. Remember to breathe slowly and deeply throughout the exercise. Don't hold your breath—many people suck in their breath when asked to contract the abdominal muscles.

The Pelvic Tilt— Muscular Control

1. Lie on your back on the floor with your knees bent.
2. Place your hands between the floor and the hollow of your back.
3. Flatten your lower back against your hands by using the stomach muscles to tilt the pelvis up and back.
4. Further tighten your stomach muscles and hold this position for five counts while breathing slowly and deeply.
5. Relax the stomach muscles and feel the pelvis roll out of the balanced position.
6. Do the exercise five times.

The Mad Cat

This second warm-up exercise helps to improve mobility and relieves stiffness and tension in the lower back.

1. Kneel on all fours with your feet pointing backwards and your hands pointing frontwards.
2. Exhale deeply and push your back from a straight position to a concave position (the opposite of the pelvic tilt). Your head and tailbone should be pointing toward the ceiling.
3. Inhale deeply and form an arch in your back by tightening the stomach and buttock muscles simultaneously so that your chin and tailbone point toward the floor. While holding this position, slowly exhale and stretch your back even further. Hold for five counts. Relax.

4. Return to the original position and do the exercise four more times.

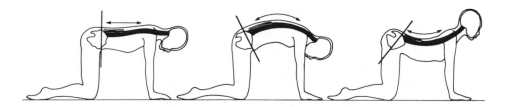

Caution

If this exercise produces discomfort, ease off and do not stretch the back to the full extreme. Gradually work up to a full stretch.

Abdominal Strengthening Exercises

Now that you're warmed up, let's move on to the Reconditioning Exercise Program.

The Curl

This exercise was designed for those who graded POOR on Test B of the National Back Fitness Test, the double straight leg raise. It allows you to practise the balanced pelvic position and increases the strength of the abdominal muscles with a minimum of back movement.

Position

1. Lie on the floor with arms at the side of the body.
2. Bend knees to a 45 degree angle and place the feet flat on the floor.

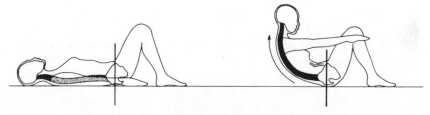

Procedure

1. Assume the pelvic tilt.
2. Inhale deeply while holding the pelvic tilt.
3. While exhaling slowly, gradually curl the head, shoulders, and upper back up off the floor. NOTE: If your feet come off the floor you are raising the body up too far.
4. Keeping the head curled in, concentrate on maintaining the pelvic tilt and hold this raised position for a slow count of five.
5. Inhale and return to the starting position.
6. Release the pelvic tilt.
7. Do the exercise five times.
8. Once you are able to easily hold the curl position for the count of five begin increasing the duration of the holding position until you can hold it for a count of ten.

Caution

Tuck your chin in while performing this exercise. Jerking the head aggressively may cause pain or discomfort in the neck. Curl up slowly and smoothly—if you try to come up too fast, you may experience lower or upper back discomfort.

Pitfalls

Do not hold your breath—coordinate your breathing properly with the exercise. Do not tuck your feet under something to help you come up (this can be harmful to a weak back). Do not attempt a full sit-up at this stage.

The Sit Back

This exercise was designed for those who graded FAIR on Tests A or B. It gradually strengthens the abdominal muscles, increases the flexibility of the lower back, and trains the individual to hold the pelvic tilt during a large arc of movement.

Position

1. Sit on the floor with your knees bent at a 45 degree angle and feet flat on the floor.
2. Stretch your arms straight out in front of you.

Procedure

1. Inhale and assume the pelvic tilt position.
2. Exhale and slowly lower your back to the floor unfolding the back so that each vertebra meets the floor in turn. NOTE: If your feet come off the floor during this exercise, roll backwards to the floor like a ball.
3. Return to the starting position by pushing yourself up with your arms.
4. Do the exercise five times.

Caution

If your feet come off the floor, it indicates a lack of spinal flexibility and you should increase the number of times you do the warm-up exercises for a few more weeks. If you feel pain during the exercise check to make sure that you are holding the pelvic tilt position.

Pitfall

Do not tuck your feet under something to hold them down. This exercises the wrong muscles and can harm a weak back.

The Bent-leg
Sit-up

This exercise was designed for those who graded GOOD on Test A or B. It further strengthens the abdominal muscles and improves the flexibility of the lower back.

Position

1. Lie on your back on the floor with knees bent to a 45 degree angle.
2. Keep your legs eight inches apart and feet flat on the floor.
3. Extend your arms in front of the body (not over the head).

Procedure

1. Take a deep breath, exhale slowly, and assume the pelvic tilt.
2. Keeping your feet flat on the floor, slowly rise to a sitting position.
3. Inhaling deeply, slowly and carefully lower your body back to the floor, curling your back with the chin held against your chest.
4. Rest and do the exercise four more times.

Caution

If you experience pain, check to make sure that you are holding the pelvic tilt throughout the exercise. If you feel a great deal of discomfort, decrease the number of repetitions.

Pitfalls

Coordinate breathing throughout the exercise and make sure to do it slowly and smoothly. There is a tendency for people to make a heroic effort to do a lot of fast sit-ups, using the momentum to help them rise. Remember that it is better to do ten slow sit-ups than 100 fast ones. If your feet keep rising off the ground, increase the warm-up exercises.

Variations

Once this exercise is easily accomplished you can challenge your muscles further by:

1. Doing the sit up with your arms crossed on your chest.

2. Later place your hands behind your neck. Remember not to jerk your head up as this will cause neck pain. Keep moving slowly and smoothly—don't push too quickly ahead.

Hip Flexor
Lengthening Exercises

Knee Kiss

This exercise is designed for those who graded POOR on Test D, the hip flexor test. It is basically a stretching exercise and can be especially useful in the morning if you awake with a stiff back. It imparts movement to the lower vertebrae and stretches back muscles that have stiffened during the night.

Position

1. Lie on your back on the floor with your head supported by a pillow.
2. Bend your legs to a 45 degree angle with feet flat on the floor.

Procedure

1. Assume the pelvic tilt while exhaling deeply.
2. Hold this position, inhale deeply and while exhaling, slowly bring one knee to your chest.
3. Grasp your knee below the kneecap and hold the knee tightly to the chest for a count of five.
4. Consciously feel your tight back muscles relax.
5. Release your leg and return it slowly to the starting position while deeply inhaling and holding the pelvic tilt.
6. Relax the pelvic tilt position.
7. Repeat movement using the other leg.

The pelvic tilt must be maintained as the leg is lowered. Remember to pull the knee gently to the chest—aggressive stretching or bouncing can cause discomfort.

Hip Stretch

This exercise was designed for those who tested FAIR on Test D, the hip flexor test. It stretches the short hip flexors and trains you in the strong balanced pelvis movement necessary for good posture.

Position

1. Lie on floor with head on a pillow, legs outstretched, and arms at your side.
2. Bend your knees at a 45 degree angle and place your feet flat on floor.

Procedure

1. Exhale deeply and assume the pelvic tilt position.
2. Holding this position, inhale deeply, then exhale and bring one knee to your chest.
3. Grasping the knee below the kneecap, hold it tightly to your chest while sliding the opposite leg straight out and stretching it to the floor.
4. Hold to a count of five. You will feel a pulling movement on the inside of the groin.
5. Return the leg back to the bent position.
6. Release and return the clasped knee to the starting position while deeply inhaling.
7. Relax the pelvic tilt position.
8. Repeat movement using the opposite leg.
9. Do the exercise five times for each leg.

Caution

Pain can result if the exercise is pursued too aggressively or too soon after an injury. Mild discomfort may result at the beginning of this exercise. If so, ease off and proceed more gradually.

Don't let your leg slip away from your chest. Hold the pelvic tilt position, especially when the opposite leg is outstretched. There is a tendency for the back to pull into an arched position, which defeats the purpose of the exercise and can be painful.

Advanced
Hip Stretch

This exercise was designed for those who graded GOOD on Test D, the hip flexors test. It stretches the hip flexors.

Position

Lie on the edge of a firm bed with both legs bent to a 45 degree angle and feet flat on the bed.

Procedure

1. Exhale deeply and assume the pelvic tilt position.
2. Grasping the knee below the kneecap bring one leg tightly to the chest and inhale deeply.
3. Exhale deeply while dangling the other leg over the edge of the bed.
4. Hold this position for a count of five and allow the dangling leg to stretch further down toward the floor.
5. Return your legs to the starting position.
6. Relax the pelvic tilt position.
7. Do the exercise five times for one leg and then switch to the other side of the bed and do it five times for the other leg

• Caution

The bent leg must be held tightly clasped to the chest or the back will arch into a vulnerable position.

Pitfalls

Do not force the dangling leg to stretch further down but let the weight of gravity pull it down. Remember to breathe out deeply as this allows the. muscles to relax and stretch.

Lateral Trunk
Muscle Exercises

The Leg Lift

This exercise is designed for those who graded POOR on Test C, the lateral trunk muscles test. It is designed to strengthen the lateral trunk and leg muscles. Many lifting injuries weaken the lateral trunk muscles, especially on the side of the back where the injury was sustained.

Position

1. Lie on the floor on your left side with your left arm comfortably supporting the head and your right arm balancing the body.
2. Make sure that your body and legs are in a straight line.

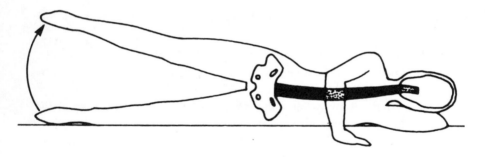

Procedure

1. Assume the pelvic tilt position.
2. Raise the upper leg slowly about 12 inches toward the ceiling.
3. Return to the original position.
4. Do the exercise ten times.
5. Turn over, lie on the right side, and do the exercise ten more times.

Pitfalls

Make sure when you raise your upper leg that the trunk of your body does not twist forward or backward. Assuming the pelvic tilt helps to stabilize the body in a straight position.

Double Leg Lift

This exercise is designed for those who graded FAIR on Test C, the lateral trunk muscles test. It will strengthen the lateral trunk and leg muscles.

Position

1. Lie on the floor on your left side, with your head comfortably supported by your left arm and your right arm balancing your body.
2. Make sure your body is in a straight line.

Procedure

1. Assume the pelvic tilt.
2. Raise both legs one inch off the floor.
3. Holding this position slowly raise the upper leg 12 inches toward the ceiling.
4. Return the upper leg slowly down to the lower leg.
5. Do the exercise five times.
6. Turn on the right side and do the exercise five times.

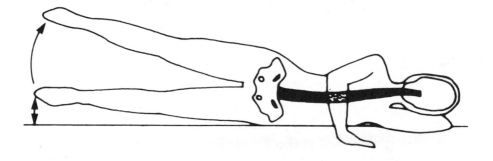

Caution

Make sure to keep the pelvic tilt position so that your body is stabilized in a straight line.

Pitfalls

Do the exercise slowly for maximum results.

Maximum
Leg Lift

This exercise is designed for those who graded GOOD on Test C, the lateral trunk muscles test. It will strengthen the lateral trunk and leg muscles.

Position

1. Lie on the floor on your left side, with your left arm comfortably supporting your head and your right arm on the floor balancing your body.
2. Make sure your body is lying in a straight line.

Procedure

1. Assume the pelvic tilt.
2. Raise both legs three inches off the floor.
3. Hold this position.
4. Slowly raise your upper leg 12 inches toward the ceiling.
5. Return the upper leg slowly back to the lower leg.
6. Repeat five times.
7. Turn and lie on your right side and repeat the exercise five times.

Pitfalls

Do not twist the body out of position. Assuming the pelvic tilt will help to keep the body in a straight line.

Scoring
the Exercises

Here's how to use the scoring chart for the reconditioning exercises.

1. Mark in your grade for the National Back Fitness Test (excellent, good, fair, or poor) in the column headed Back Muscle Grading.
2. Each day after you exercise mark the number of times you did the exercise under the appropriate day—for example, Sat 10.
3. At the end of the week go back to the chapter on the National Back Fitness Test, retest yourself and mark down your score.
4. If your grade has improved move on to the next level of exercise.

5. If your grade remains the same, perform the exercise series *twice*. Do *not* just increase the number of repetitions of each exercise—this could strain the muscles. Go through each set of exercises five times. Then repeat them from beginning to end.

6. At the end of the second week retest yourself. If your grade has not improved, repeat the series of exercises three times instead of twice. By the end of the third week your grade should have improved if you have performed the exercises properly and conscientiously each day.

The National Back
Fitness Regrading Test

	Back Muscle Grading	Sun	Mon	Tues	Wed	Thurs	Fri	Sat	Back Fitness Test Regrading
Test A The Sit-up (Flexibility)									
Test B Double Straight Leg Raise (Abdominal Strength)									
Test C Lateral Trunk Lift (Trunk and Leg Strength)	L								
	R								
Test D The Hip Flexors (Hip Flexor Length)	L								
	R								

No Pain
Allowed

During the first few days of a new exercise, some muscle stiffness may develop. This is natural and to be expected. Muscle stiffness is different from acute pain. You've felt stiffness in the past when you attempted a new sport for the first time. But if you are feeling pain when you exercise, take a look at the following checklist.

- Are you holding the pelvic tilt throughout the exercise?
- Are you doing the exercise correctly?

- Have you overestimated your score and placed yourself at too high a level?
- Are you doing too many repeats of the exercise?
- Are you adding new exercises too quickly?
- Are you skipping the warm-up exercises?

If nothing on the checklist applies to you and you continue to feel back pain while performing the reconditioning exercises, discontinue the program and make an appointment to see your doctor.

8

The Basic Back Maintenance Program

When you have finally achieved a score of excellent on the National Back Fitness Test there will be a natural temptation to let up. After all, you've won the battle, haven't you? Yes, but only up to the first frontier of fitness. Now that your back muscles are in terrific shape how are you going to keep them that way? Remember what we said earlier about the body: it's the only machine that wears out with disuse and improves with use. In other words, use it or lose it! To keep fit you must continue to actively exercise muscles.

The back maintenance program that follows is designed to keep your back fit. I define fit as ready for action. Think about the people you know who are in good physical shape. What qualities do they possess that the unfit person doesn't have? Stamina comes first to my mind—the ability to work and play for long periods without fatigue. Coupled with stamina you will usually find slimness. The reason these two qualities go hand in hand is fairly obvious. People who can work for long periods of time without excessive fatigue are burning off a lot of calories. The same goes for play—people with endurance can swim, jog, hike, or play squash longer and harder. They can eat huge meals after one of these workouts and never gain an ounce.

The next two qualities that come to mind when discussing fitness are strength and flexibility. We know that muscles that aren't used lose both of these capabilities. True fitness, therefore, consists of four balanced qualities: stamina and slimness balanced with strength and flexibility. To cope successfully in a society that does not provide the means to develop true fitness through our work, we must counter its effects with a daily session of exercises that will replace and replenish what our bodies are missing.

The following exercises can be done in just a few minutes each day; they provide a safe, simple, and efficient method to achieve a lifetime of fitness.

Arm Circles

This exercise is designed to stretch the muscles of the shoulder girdle. Although the shoulders are capable of a very large range of movement, typists and business people who work in offices use limited arm movements during the working day. Because this type of work does not properly maintain the use of the shoulder muscles, there can be degeneration of the joints leading to arthritis in the shoulder. People with rounded shoulders because of improper posture also tend to have contracted and shortened breast or chest muscles that need stretching.

Position

1. Stand comfortably with your feet two feet apart.
2. Dangle your arms loosely at your sides.

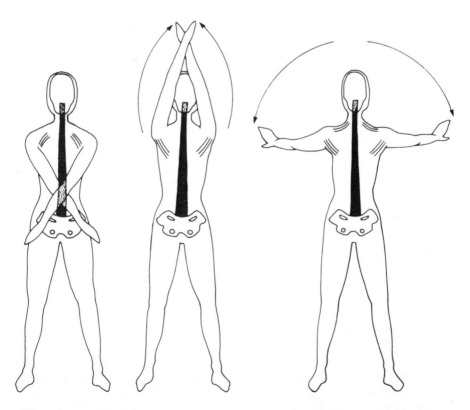

Procedure

1. Inhale slowly and deeply and cross both arms across the front of your body, feeling the stretch in your back shoulder blades.
2. Slowly lift your crossed arms up over your head (similar to the movement you make when you yawn).
3. Breathing in and then exhaling, slowly lower both arms in an arc behind your body, feeling the stretch in your chest muscles.
4. Do the exercise five to ten times.

Pitfalls

Remember to coordinate your breathing throughout the exercise and don't move the arms like a windmill—do it slowly and deliberately.

Lateral Stretch
Relaxation

This exercise balances the lateral leg lift, which is a power-strength exercise, by stretching the lateral trunk muscles.

Position

1. Stand comfortably, with feet two feet apart.
2. Let arms hang loosely at your sides.

Procedure

1. Inhale and then, slowly exhaling, slide your right arm down the side of the leg toward the knee. Stop when resistance is felt on the opposite side of the body.
2. Inhale and then exhale deeply and feel the muscles on the left side slightly relax. Stretch a little farther and hold for five counts.
3. Return to original position.
4. Do the exercise five times.
5. Do it on other side of the body five times.

Pitfalls

Do not do the exercise too quickly and remember to coordinate your breathing.

Calf
Stretch

This exercise stretches a key postural muscle. People who wear high heels all day or jog without performing compensating stretching exercises often have shortened calf muscles.

Position

1. Stand comfortably with your hands on your hips.
2. Place one foot in front of your body and one foot behind so that your feet are about one foot apart, and your toes are pointing forward.

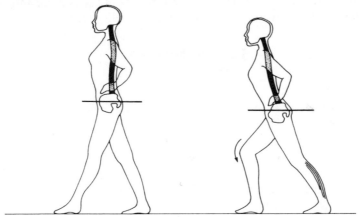

Procedure

1. Inhale deeply and then exhale slowly while lowering your body by bending the front knee.
2. Keep your back leg straight and your foot flat on the floor.
3. Feel the stretch in the calf muscle of the back leg.
4. Hold the position for five counts, inhale, and then exhale deeply and feel the muscle relax. Stretch a little farther, and again hold for five counts.
5. Do the exercise five times for each leg.

Pitfalls

Make sure that your back foot remains on the floor and your heel does not raise up. You should feel a stretch, not pain, in the calf muscle.

Quad
Stretch

This exercise is designed to strengthen the anterior thigh muscles by isometric muscular contraction. Strong thigh muscles are necessary to protect the back while you are lifting heavy objects.

Position

1. Stand with your back and buttocks against the wall and your feet comfortably (one-and-a-half to two feet) away from the wall.
2. Keep your feet apart and hands at your sides.

Procedure

1. Bend your legs at the knee and allow your back to rest on the wall so that the body seems to be resting in an imaginary chair. Your thighs should be at right angles to the wall.
2. Hold this position until the muscles tire, approximately one to two minutes.
3. Do the exercises five times.

Racer
Stretch

This exercise is designed to lengthen the hip flexors, which when shortened prevent the proper holding of the pelvic tilt and contribute to poor posture.

Position

1. Stand comfortably.
2. Lower your body all the way down to a squatting position, keeping your left foot flat on the floor.
3. Place the palms of your hands flat on the floor on each side of the left foot.
4. Extend your right leg backwards as far as possible resting your weight on your toes with the rest of the weight of your trunk on the left thigh with your left foot flat on the ground.

Procedure

1. Inhale deeply and then exhale while simultaneously allowing the weight of your trunk to rest heavily on the left knee while your right leg stretches as far back as possible.
2. Hold for a count of five. Feel the right groin stretch as your body is carried down and forward by gravity.
3. Relax and rest in this position.
4. Do the exercise five times.
5. Do it five times using other leg.

Caution

Make sure that your trunk and back are supported by the thigh and leg so that your back is not strained.

Pitfalls

Keep the forward foot flat on the floor during the exercise. Stretching must take place while exhaling for maximum benefit.

The Mad
Cat

This exercise helps improve mobility and relieves stiffness and tension in the lower back. You will remember it was a warm-up exercise that you did prior to the reconditioning exercises.

Procedure

1. Kneel on all fours with your feet pointing backwards and your hands pointing frontwards.

2. Exhale deeply and push your back from a straight position to a concave position (the opposite of the pelvic tilt). Your head and tailbone should be pointing toward the ceiling.
3. Inhale deeply and form an arch in your back by tightening the stomach and buttock muscles simultaneously so that your chin and tailbone point toward the floor. While holding this position, slowly exhale and stretch your back even further. Hold for five counts. Relax.
4. Return to the original position and do the exercise four more times.

Caution

If this exercise produces discomfort, ease off and do not stretch the back to the full extreme. Gradually work up to a full stretch.

Proper
Push-up

Push-ups strengthen the muscles of the shoulder girdle.

Position

1. Lie face down with palms of your hands flat on the floor under your shoulders.

Procedure

1. Keeping your body perfectly straight and rigid, slowly push the body away from the floor while exhaling.
2. Hold your body in this position and then inhale and return to the floor. NOTE: If it is not possible for you to hold your body straight out to the toes, use the knees as the pivot point. This position is usually preferred for women.

Pitfalls

Do not allow your body to sag or bend and do the push-ups slowly—better 10 slow than 20 fast ones. Do not hold your breath while you are performing the push-ups, but breathe *out* while pushing your body away from the floor and *in* while lowering your body to the floor.

Groin
Stretch

This exercise is designed to improve the flexibility of the lower back and the hip adductor muscles on the inside of the thigh and groin.

Position

1. Sit on the floor with your back straight, the soles of your feet touching, and your knees extended like a frog.
2. Rest your elbows on your knees to help push them outward.

Procedure

1. Deeply inhale and then exhale and allow your head to fall towards your feet while curling your upper body forward.
2. Once you feel resistance hold for five counts. Do not force your head down or to the point where you feel pain.
3. Take another deep breath in and slowly exhale and stretch the muscles in the back and groin a bit further. Hold for five counts.
4. Do the exercise five times.

Hamstring Stretch

This exercise improves the flexibility of the hamstring muscles at the back of the thigh.

Position

1. Sit on the floor with your legs stretched out in front of you.
2. Bring your right foot up and place it opposite your left knee so that the sole of your right foot is against the inside of your left knee.
3. Curl your upper body toward your left knee while reaching toward your left foot with your hands.
4. As you meet resistance when you stretch forward, take a deep breath in, then exhale and ease your body forward coming closer to the knee.
5. Hold this position for five counts.
6. Do the exercise five times.
7. Do it five times for the opposite leg.

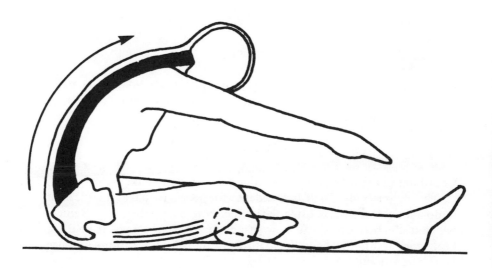

Caution

Do not bounce or strain. If the exercise is painful, ease off and proceed more gently.

The Bent-leg
Sit-up

This exercise strengthens the abdominal muscles and improves the flexibility of the lower back. It is one of the exercises you learned while reconditioning.

Position

1. Lie on your back on the floor with your knees bent to a 45 degree angle.
2. Keep your legs eight inches apart and feet flat on the floor.
3. Extend your arms in front of your body (not over your head).

Procedure

1. Take a deep breath, exhale slowly, and assume the pelvic tilt.
2. Keeping your feet flat on the floor, slowly rise to a sitting position.
3. Inhaling deeply, slowly and carefully lower your body back to the floor, curling fully back into the pelvic tilt position, with the chin held against the chest.
4. Rest and do the exercise four more times.

Caution

If you experience pain, check to make sure that you are holding the pelvic tilt throughout the exercise. If you feel a great deal of discomfort, decrease the number of repetitions.

Pitfalls

Coordinate breathing throughout the exercise and make sure to do it slowly and smoothly. There is a tendency for people to make a heroic effort to do a lot of fast sit-ups, using the momentum to help them rise. Remember that it is better to do 10 slow sit-ups than 100 fast ones. If your feet keep coming off the floor, increase the number of warm-up exercises you've been doing.

Variations

You can challenge your muscles further by:

1. Doing the sit-up with your arms crossed on your chest.

2. Later place your hands behind your neck. Remember not to jerk your head up as this will cause neck pain. Keep moving slowly and smoothly—don't push too quickly ahead.

Maximum
Leg Lift

This exercise is one you learned to strengthen your lateral trunk and leg muscles.

Position

1. Lie on the floor on your left side with your left arm comfortably supporting your head and your right arm balancing your body.
2. Make sure your body is lying in a straight line.

Procedure

1. Assume the pelvic tilt.
2. Raise both legs six inches off the floor.
3. Hold this position.
4. Slowly raise the upper leg as far toward the ceiling as possible.
5. Return the upper leg slowly back to the lower leg.
6. Do the exercise five times.
7. Turn and lie on your right side and do it five times.

Pitfalls

Do not twist the body out of position. Assuming the pelvic tilt will help to keep the body in a straight line.

Performed quickly, these simple exercises will help your back stay fit. They are easy, safe, and a great warm-up before playing any sport. They are also excellent tension relievers after a hard day over a hot desk. A combination of isometric and isotonic movements, they can be used to rev up in the morning or tone down and relax at night. Take your pick—but do them daily. They only take ten minutes. Remember consistency is the key to fitness.

9

Going Straight: The Importance of Posture

When it comes to posture I'm a nag. My children complain that my preoccupation with the subject makes them feel as if they are living with a maiden aunt. In self-defence, I try to explain that there's a good reason for my concern—I don't want them to end up with chronic backache.

There was a time when I was amazed at the foggy notions my back patients had about good posture. Now I just assume that it's not high on most people's list of priorities. They are far more interested in losing weight. Posture is simply not part of modern body image. And because posture has not been emphasized in schools and physical education classes, most people who stand incorrectly are sublimely unaware of the fact. They are also uninformed about the way poor posture can affect their health and good looks.

Let me put you to the test. If I asked you to stand up straight what would you do? Well, if you're like the majority of my patients you would immediately adopt a military stance with the shoulders thrust back as far as possible and the chest and chin pushed forward. Now, I don't know where this mistaken idea of good posture sprang from—maybe your parents were to blame for urging you to keep your shoulders held back or perhaps you spent a few years in a cadet school. What I do know, however, is that the at-attention way of standing is not good posture. In fact, it's an unnatural and forced way to hold the body, one which will cause pain and fatigue if maintained for long periods of time.

As I've already explained, there is little point in advising people to stand up straight when the abdominal muscles are too weak and the psoas muscles too short to hold the pelvis in the proper position to keep the spine erect. My major objective so far has been to show you how to recondition your back muscles—and how to keep them in condition—so that you have the potential to change your posture. Good postural habits will prevent back fatigue and make the back less vulnerable to injury. As a bonus, you'll look 100 per cent more attractive.

So let's examine just what good posture is and how it can be developed. Because it's qualitative rather than quantitative, posture is hard to measure, but I'm going to try to define it anyhow. I think of good posture as a state of optimal balance. Posture is the body's expression of the work being done by the muscles to hold it erect against the forces of gravity. Good posture exists when all parts of the body are held in a state of balance so that the supporting boney structures are protected from injury and the muscles from fatigue.

Posture is not solely a manifestation of physical balance—it's also an expression of mental balance. Think about the way you stand when you are depressed or tired: you stand with your shoulders rounded and drooping. Your body represents your emotions by giving up the fight against gravity, sagging just as low as you feel. When you're feeling good your body also expresses your emotions. "I'm on my toes," you'll say. A friend who's adept at body language will be able to see when everything is rosy by the way you're standing: tall, head up, ready to take on all comers. It's also notable that the term "well-balanced" is used to describe someone who "won't go over the edge" and whose emotions are "on an even keel."

Mankind has always had to struggle to achieve a balanced state of mind. So, too, the body has had to fight against gravity every moment of the day to remain erect and balanced. Because our bodies are much like inverted triangles, with the feet forming the narrow base of support and the centre of gravity located high in the pelvic area, all that prevents us from falling is muscular action. It follows, therefore, that the better our posture, the less work the muscles need to do to hold us erect.

Good posture hinges on the pelvic tilt. When the body is held in this position, the back curves normally and the muscles are the optimal working length so that no single group of them is forced to work overtime to hold us up. Do you remember the analogy used earlier in the book in which the lower spine was compared to a ship's mast? I suggested that the lower spine, the working unit of the back, sits on the pelvic foundation much as a mast sits on a deck. Just as the mast is moored to the deck by guy wires, so the lower spine is attached to the pelvic floor by back muscles. If any of those muscles are stretched or sagging the other muscles, like the guy wires holding up the ship's mast, must take up the stress or pull so that the spine will continue to be held erect. When a person has an excessively curved back or poor posture, certain groups of muscles are stretched out of position, past the optimal working length, and other muscles have to take up the extra load. For example, if the abdominal muscles are weak, the pelvis is shifted forward, causing the back and psoas muscles to be over-used in an effort to take up the slack. This over-loading sets up chronic fatigue, which can lead to backache.

The Mirror Test

Convincing my patients that faulty posture is hard on their backs can be a difficult job. It's even harder to demonstrate just what faulty posture is. Usually I have to show people how to look in a mirror. The following case history illustrates my point.

The Case of Paul N. Age 19

I could see my young receptionist's eyes light up when Paul came to my office for a pre-employment physical. It must have been a nice change for her to see a young, handsome man stride into the clinic, instead of the usual back patient. No matter what their age, they tend to look pretty decrepit, hobbling in, all bent over with back spasms. A year-round athlete who played basketball, volleyball, and baseball, Paul appeared to be in terrific physical shape. Nevertheless, the job he had applied for involved manual labour and his employer wanted him to take the National Back Fitness Test. He believed Paul had the right to know whether he was going to be able to physically handle the job.

Paul certainly had no doubts, just as he had no problems with the first three parts of the fitness test. Because of his superbly conditioned abdominal muscles, the sit-ups, double leg raises, and lateral side lifts were a breeze for him. It was during the hip flexors test that the first indication of trouble showed up. Paul could not keep either leg flat on the examining table when the opposite knee was pulled to his chest. The power-strength exercises required for Paul's sports activities had shortened his hip flexors because he'd done no stretch-relaxation exercises to compensate. In turn, these tight hip flexors had affected his posture.

But posture had little meaning for Paul. When I asked him to check the way he stood, he faced the mirror straight on, studied his image and said, "I think I stand okay."

"How about taking a look at yourself from a different angle?" I suggested. "Stand sideways and tell me what you now see in the mirror." I watched Paul as he studied himself. Like most of my patients, he had no conception of posture. His eyes immediately focussed on his flat stomach but he ignored his shoulders and back. "Paul, have you ever noticed that your shoulders are slightly rounded? And take a look at your back. Can you see how exaggerated the curve is in the small of your back?"

"I never really noticed it before," Paul confessed.

"That exaggerated curve is called hyperlordosis and it's an indicator of poor posture—you're not standing correctly."

"But I've never had any problems," Paul said. "So what difference does it make how I stand?"

"Okay, Paul, I'm going to give you a demonstration that might convince you. Let's examine those shoulder muscles of yours." Many people with rounded shoulders have tense, rigid shoulder muscles and Paul was no exception. His muscles were so rigid with painful nodules or trigger points near the base of the neck that, when I probed them with my thumbs, he winced. "Your muscles are so tight up there Paul that they actually feel more like bone than muscle. Tell me, do you get many headaches?"

"Yeah, I was away from school a lot during the past year because of bad headaches."

"Right. I want to try something with you: I want you to stand with your stomach tucked in, the hollow of your back flattened, shoulders slightly back, your head up, and eyes straight ahead." When Paul was in this position of balanced posture I once more probed the trigger points in his shoulders. "How does it feel now?" I asked him.

"Gee, it hardly hurts at all now. How come?"

I explained that when he was standing up straight his shoulder muscles were relaxed, allowing the blood to circulate more freely in the muscles and flush away the built-up toxic wastes. I suggested it was possible his headaches were caused by the constricted shoulder muscles and, if this were the cause, good posture would go a long way toward minimizing them. "Can you understand now how poor posture can effect your health, Paul?" I asked.

"I get the point," Paul said. "I'm going to try and stand up straight from now on."

"You won't be able to stand up straight unless you stretch your hip flexor muscles," I told him. "All the mental effort in the world won't change your posture if the muscles aren't in the right shape to hold the spine up."

"All right, tell me what to do and I'll work on those muscles. But I have the feeling the posture bit is going to be a tougher problem than the muscle stretching."

"Why's that?"

"It's like this, doctor: it feels kind of funny when I stand up straight. I'm so used to the wrong way that the right way feels wrong."

The Right Way Feels Wrong

I knew exactly what Paul meant. If you've been holding your body incorrectly for years it has become second nature to you—it feels right. That's because posture is a habit. But you weren't born with bad posture. Although posture is an unconscious and involuntary activity maintained automatically by reflex actions, it's a learned activity. You developed your postural habits while you were growing and your muscles were developing. When a baby is born it cannot hold its head or body erect. As the muscles develop, the child learns to hold its head up, to crawl, then stand, walk, and run. Toddlers have pot bellies and pronounced bodily curves because their muscles have not fully developed. It isn't until puberty that the muscles begin to fully develop and posture becomes fixed.

However, this fixed posture that will carry over to adulthood is influenced by more than the strength of the muscles: children also pattern posture on that of parents and peer group. The earliest influences are the parents but as children grow older they imitate private heroes and, in the teenage years, peers.

It is during the crucial teenage years that bad posture can take over for good. The adolescent who has always been shy will become permanently fixed in the habit of walking with the head hanging down to avoid meeting anybody's eyes. A defensive, round-shouldered approach to life is often displayed by teenagers suffering from an inferiority complex, just as youngsters, embarrassed about their height and gawkiness, will slump in an effort to appear more like their classmates (it's especially difficult for a girl who is head and shoulders above the boys in her class). Another prime candidate for bad posture is the girl who is selfconscious about her developing breasts—she will hunch her shoulders together and slump in an attempt to hide her chest. This is also a period when boys and girls have a desperate need to be accepted by their group. If a slouch is the accepted posture of the "in" crowd, the kids will copy it.

What, then, is a parent to do if a child develops poor posture? There are no easy answers. Teenagers are notoriously unwilling to accept parental suggestions—in fact, to assert their independence they will often take a diametrically opposed course of action. As most parents of teenagers will wearily agree, it requires a certain amount of guile to persuade them to do anything that's good for them. Still, teenagers are extremely selfconscious about their looks. Sometimes an appeal to their vanity, if made indirectly and subtly, can bring a change in their posture. The best solution, though, is to set an example while they are small. The earliest influences on a child are the most profound and if parents practice good posture they can be fairly certain their children will also stand correctly.

Beauty and
the Back

Rightly or wrongly, we live in a society that places a tremendous value on youthful good looks. We are a nation obsessed with dieting to look slim and young. We spend countless hours in beauty salons trying to achieve perfect complexions and beautiful hair. We spend thousands of dollars on the newest clothing styles. And it's all okay with me. Why shouldn't we try to look good? The trouble is that we sometimes forget that true beauty depends on line and form, as much as on accoutrements.

Why do we instinctively appreciate the beauty of a thoroughbred race-horse or a high-powered sports car? It's the combination of line and movement that makes us acknowledge their excellence. It's the same with people. Someone who moves well and whose body is in alignment gives an impression of elegance and vitality that is always impressive. That's why dancers and models must undergo rigorous training to learn how to hold themselves gracefully. It's movement that creates the impression of beauty and because movement is an expression of the personality, we automatically judge people by the way they stand and walk.

Posture is also the criterion by which we judge age: someone with a bent back who moves slowly and carefully is considered old while someone who stands erectly and moves with confidence is considered young for that age.

I think most of us have a healthy amount of vanity in our souls—we'd all like to look younger, more graceful, and elegant. Learning how to stand and move correctly can take us a long way toward those goals. And although it's a difficult message to get across to children, it's worth the trouble. Concerned parents will spend a small fortune on braces so their children will have straight teeth and captivating smiles, but correcting bad postural habits will also go a long way toward helping them become healthy, beautiful, and energetic adults.

Test
Your Posture

How does your posture rate? Your mirror will tell you the good or bad news. Stand sideways in front of a full-length mirror and prepare to view your body dispassionately. I know it can be a dismaying sight but comfort

THE PLUMB LINE SHOWING GOOD POSTURE

THE PLUMB LINE SHOWING POOR POSTURE

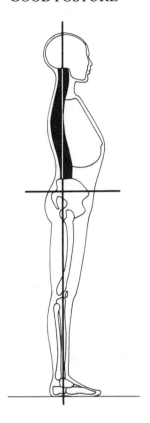
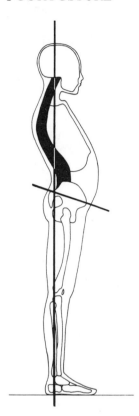

yourself with the thought that in a few weeks time, you're going to look a whole lot better.

Now try to imagine a plumb line hanging from the ceiling; it represents a line of force through the body's centre of gravity. The line should fall behind the ear, the nape of the neck, the base of the back behind the hip, in front of the knee, and down through the bone in the ankle. You can see the way the line should descend in the accompanying diagram.

If your body falls primarily behind or in front of the line, you have poor posture. Check the following: How great a degree is your spine curved from the line? Do you have rounded shoulders? Is your head carried forward and drooping? How about your lumbar curve? Is it exaggerated? Is your abdomen protruding? Do your buttocks stick out?

I grant that these are not particularly appetizing facts for anyone to face. Who needs it? No wonder people prefer to view themselves while facing straight on—almost everyone looks better that way. But that won't show up your postural defects so they can be corrected. Remember that posture is a habit and habits can be changed. Bad posture can be unlearned and good posture can become automatic. If you consciously practice good posture, in a very short while it will become unconscious.

Make a Habit of It

Good posture centres on the pelvic tilt. Put your pelvis into the balanced position and the natural curves in your back reduce to a minumum.

If you want to see just how much your spine straightens out when you're in the balanced pelvic position, try this test. Stand in your normal posture against a wall and have a friend mark your height with a pencil. Now assume the pelvic tilt. Tuck in your stomach, press the small of your back as flat as you can against the wall, pull your shoulders slightly back and hold your head up. You will discover that you have just grown an inch, sometimes two. When a patient of mine adopted good postural habits he told me it was creating a problem for him at work—it made him look too much like the boss.

Once you have become aware that the pelvic tilt is the key to good posture, you should practice it until it becomes a habit. I advise my patients to take a visual cue—for example, every time you walk through a doorway you should check to see if you're holding yourself in the balanced pelvic position. With a little motivation and some self-discipline it won't take long until good posture becomes a part of your life and something you no longer need to think about.

Now let's get on to good postural habits while sitting and lying down. It may come as surprise to learn that good posture is important while you are sleeping. But if you realize that it's only during sleep that the back gets a chance to rest completely, you can see how important it is to lie in a way that promotes total relaxation of the spine. That's why you should always avoid sleeping on your stomach; it causes the back to arch so the vertebrae are stressed. You know how uncomfortable your wrist would feel if it were held in an extreme position for several hours. The back reacts in the same way and after a night spent sleeping on your stomach, it could feel painful and stiff when you wake. Sleep, instead, on your side with the knees and hips bent as much as is comfortable, allowing the spine to relax. If you feel more comfortable lying on your back, support your knees and hips by resting them on pillows so that the back is put into the balanced pelvic position.

Good sitting posture depends on two simple rules. The first is to sit so that the knees are higher than the hips. The second rule is to ensure that the lower back is well supported. Crossing one knee over the other is a simple way to get the knees higher than the hips and to automatically roll the pelvis into the proper balanced position. Try it and you will feel the small of your back push into the back of the chair. Uncross your legs and notice how the back arches into a more stressed and curved posture. When you are sitting at a desk, put a book or box under the desk as a footrest. Your knees will then be higher than your hips and the spine will be stretched and relaxed. While you're watching TV at night put your feet up. Actually, most people do this automatically when they want to relax. They might not know much about the pelvic tilt position but they realize that sitting with the feet up feels comfortable.

If you must stand for long periods of time, place one foot on a stool or box to tilt the pelvis into a balanced position. Your spine will feel less fatigue. Have you ever noticed that all standing bars have foot rails? That's because a drinker will be able to relax and, the bar owner hopes, take the time to quaff a few more.

Every method of producing good posture while standing, walking, sitting, or lying down is one that puts the pelvis into a balanced position so the spine can relax. When you assume the pelvic tilt you are able to rest your back even while you work. When you don't practice good posture you make your back work even while it rests.

10

Lifting
Can Be a Pain
in the Back

We have already seen how the human machine, designed by nature to work effectively through the constant exercise of the muscles, can get fouled up in a technological society. The epidemic of back ailments in North America is just one result of our high-tech way of life. And as we have also learned, almost everyone blames back injuries on lifting things the wrong way.

Although a primary cause of back trouble is, of course, weak back muscles, it is possible to get along without problems as long as those weak muscles are not called upon to perform beyond their capacity. If, however, they are suddenly required to take on a heavy job of lifting, watch out! Even when the back muscles are in good working shape, lifting something awkwardly can hurt the back because the stresses and loads are placed upon the wrong part of the spine.

Well aware of the hazards involved in unsafe lifting, industries plaster office and factory walls with posters urging employees to use proper techniques. They also offer intensive training programs on the subject. So far, this hasn't solved the problem. That's where the Back Care Centre came into the picture. Even though this book has focussed primarily on the needs of individuals, it should be remembered that the clinic was established in response to the demands of industry. As aware as they are of the significance to their bottom lines, many companies are still unable to deal with the problems caused by lifting accidents.

A small trucking company that approached me a few years ago offers an example of the difficulties involved. It employed 225 workers and had been very successful in attracting new business during its early years because of a progressive management that had kept the truck fleet running at top capacity. Although most aspects of the business were going smoothly, employee absenteeism was high and beginning to cause trouble. Schedules were being missed and customers were complaining about late deliveries. An analysis of company records showed that 80% of the absenteeism was caused by back problems, many of them attributed to lifting accidents. Aside from the negative effects on productivity, the company comptroller was upset about the costs—more than $1,300 a year for each employee.

The company did indeed have a problem, but why were they unable to handle it? When they sent me one of their employees who had developed a recurring back problem, the reasons became obvious.

The Case of Charlie G.
Age 35

A very hostile Charlie met me in my clinic. "I'm only here because the company insisted that I see you," he started out. "I've got my own doctor and he's a damn good one. He's made a full report to the company about my back problem. What's the matter? Don't they believe him?"

I tried to reassure him that my sole purpose in seeing him was to try to help him with his back pain, but I could see he remained unconvinced. Charlie had first hurt his back six months before while lifting a heavy wheel-barrow on the job. He returned to work two weeks later but his back was stiff when he woke up in the mornings and it continued to bother him. Because he was aware that his back was not in very good shape he had attempted to conscientiously practice the safe lifting techniques advised by the company, but three months after the first accident he again "threw his back out" while lifting a load from a truck. The second accident had kept him off work for three months and his recovery had been slow and painful. Because he was still suffering from a nagging backache his doctor had requested that the company put him on lighter duties.

"The older guys are really resentful that I'm not slugging it out the way they are," Charlie told me. "And the foreman isn't feeling too sympathetic either—my time off increased his work load all summer and he sure lets me know it. The boss is browned off—he's told me, very subtly, of course—that I cost the company a lot of money. Everybody's acting like I wanted the damn accident. The safety inspector came right out and said that if I'd been lifting the right way, the accident would never have happened. Do they actually believe anyone wants to lie around for three months in the kind of pain I was in? I kept thinking about my dad. He had bad back problems and he ended up pensioned off when he was only 48. I'm beginning to wonder if it's going to be that way for me too."

No wonder Charlie was feeling upset and no wonder the company was frustrated about back problems. When a "blame situation" is set up, effective communication is impossible. Management worries about the adverse effects of back problems on their production schedules and profits; unions regard back problems as reactions to a hostile working environment; employees feel they must expend as much effort proving that the job caused the problem as in trying to get better. The tension caused by these conflicting viewpoints is exacerbated by the underlying assumption that accidents are the result of either unsafe conditions or unsafe acts. Thus both management and worker take a defensive stance and try to prove who is in the wrong instead of working together to solve the problem.

Safe Lifting

At the Back Care Centre we have a different point of view: we emphasize that back problems result from a mismatch between the worker's capability and the demands of the task. We try to show that they can be solved only if all interested parties make a joint effort to resolve the resulting absenteeism. We stress that the problem must be viewed from three angles:

1. Is the worker's back fit enough to handle a specific job?
2. Are equipment and other environmental factors in the work place adequately designed?
3. Is there proper on-the-job training in lifting techniques and back care principle?

Because the back must be in good enough shape to handle the task, we stress the need for strengthening exercises as well as knowledge of safe lifting principles.

Let's review the traditional rules of safe lifting, and then we'll examine the reasons behind the rules and why they are sometimes ignored at high cost to both worker and employee.

The Traditional Rules

Various methods of safe lifting and material handling are taught in industry. These methods commonly stress that a worker should:

- size up the load before attempting the lift
- balance with feet wide apart
- bend the knees
- keep the back straight
- grip the object firmly
- hold the load close to the body
- avoid twisting

All these rules are important but, unfortunately, some of them do not come naturally to a lot of people. For example, people whose muscles are so weak that their backs cannot be held in an erect position long enough to perform a lifting task will not benefit from advice to keep their backs straight. And while avoiding twisting is essential to protect the lower spine, it is better to show *how* to avoid twisting than merely to say not to do it. At the Back Care Centre we have found it effective to explain the simple principles behind the rules and show the employee how to apply them.

When the traditional safe lifting rules are re-examined, they can be boiled down to one key factor: *adopt the balanced pelvic position or pelvic tilt during the lift*. This position automatically straightens the back, makes it impossible for the spine to twist, makes it necessary to bend the knees instead of the back (because the back cannot be bent all the way over) and allows the abdominal cavity to distribute the forces of the lift equally in all directions and save the spine from excessive stress.

Pelvic Tilt
Lifting

A reminder: the spine has two major components, each with a different function:

- The stable vertebral bodies and discs at the front of the spinal column are designed to transmit weight and force;
- The delicate facet joints at the back of the vertebrae provide flexibility and spinal movement.

Safe lifting requires that the force be transmitted through the solid vertebral bodies. The discs between the vertebral bodies function as shock absorbers and the weight of the load does not strain the back. This occurs only when the back is in the pelvic tilt. However, if the back is in the excessively curved position of poor posture, the force of the lift falls on the facet joints. Since they are not designed to bear weight, the back is vulnerable to strain and injury. Poor posture also causes wedging of the vertebrae, abnormal stress on the discs, and a narrowing of the space where the spinal nerves exit from the spinal cord—all factors making the spine vulnerable while lifting. If the back is stabilized in the pelvic tilt, safe lifting techniques become automatic. You don't have to consciously think about their application. Try it yourself and feel the difference between traditional lifting and pelvic tilt lifting.

1. Find an object of 20 to 35 pounds that is fairly easy to handle and place it on the floor.
2. Stand close to the object, with your feet spread comfortably apart.
3. Bend your knees.
4. Keep your back straight.
5. Grip the object firmly.
6. Lift it.

Now repeat the procedure.

1. Tilt your pelvis into the balanced position.
2. Bend your knees.
3. Keep your back straight.
4. Grip the object firmly.
5. Tighten your stomach muscles.
6. Lift the object while maintaining a strong contraction of the stomach muscles.

PELVIC TILT LIFTING

By following this sequence you are using your back at its strongest. The key to handling materials safely is to maintain good posture whether you are lifting, pushing, pulling, or carrying. For continuous heavy work you must be in good physical condition but the practice of good postural habits will make any job easier and less fatiguing.

Here's another example that demonstrates how the pelvic tilt protects the back while lifting:

1. Stand with your feet ten inches apart.
2. Tighten your stomach muscles and hold the pelvic tilt.
3. Twist from your waist while holding the pelvic tilt.
4. Notice that to twist past 45 degrees you must gradually let go of the pelvic tilt. To twist 100 degrees to 180 degrees you must release the pelvis into the opposite weak position and allow the spine to curve.

It is easy to forget the "don't twist while lifting" rule if you are not using your back properly, but if the pelvic tilt is maintained, the back will "remember" for you. The muscles will not allow the spine to be used in a weak, vulnerable position.

Hydraulic Sac
Principle

When you tuck in and use the pelvic tilt, you automatically gain an advantage—the abdominal cavity becomes a hydraulic sac.

In a sense, the hydraulic sac acts something like a water bed, dispersing the weight evenly in all directions and relieving the spine of extra pressure. A water bed is capable of supporting tremendous weight—a 200 pound man, for example. When the man lies on the water bed, his weight exerts a great deal of outward force on the fluid and air inside the bed. But because it is an enclosed sac, the walls of the water bed exert an equal and opposite resistance to the force of the weight. It provides a stable and strong surface that absorbs the force and stress placed upon it.

Similarly, the abdominal cavity can resist a great deal of external force, but only if it is stabilized by muscular action in the strong pelvic tilt posture. If the posture is poor and the stomach muscles weak, the muscles are unable to sustain the tension required to effectively support the spine. The greatest force falls directly on the spine rather than being distributed evenly over the entire abdominal cavity.

When the back is in the pelvic tilt, the stomach and trunk muscles automatically contract. This contraction stabilizes the abdominal cavity and enables it to act like a water bed, distributing forces equally in all directions. The spine is supported rather than weakened and the lifting forces are distributed over a larger area. When the back is held in a position of good posture, the spine itself is required to withstand only a relatively small portion of the load.

The following procedures demonstrate how the hydraulic sac principle works:

1. Stand with your stomach muscles relaxed.
2. Bend forward, holding your upper body at a 45 degree angle from your legs.
3. Hold this position for a count of ten.
4. Notice how quickly your back tires.

Try repeating this procedure, but this time use an enclosed sac, such as a basketball, or soccer or beach ball, to support the back.

1. Stand holding the ball in front of you.
2. Bend your knees slightly.
3. Press the ball firmly against your abdomen.
4. Lean forward to a 45 degree angle, continuing to press the ball against your abdomen.
5. Feel how your muscles automatically contract and absorb the force of bending forward and relieve the pressure on the back.

The hydraulic sac lifting technique requires the abdominal cavity to be used, just as the ball is used in this demonstration, to distribute the forces of the lift and stabilize the back.

Pelvic tilt lifting does not come naturally at first. The back and stomach muscles need training to hold the balanced pelvic position under lifting stress. If you practice lifting in the pelvic tilt, the technique will become natural and the stomach muscles will increase in fitness and endurance.

Awkward Lifts

There are always occasions when the rules of safe lifting cannot be applied. For instance, you can't bend your knees and get close to the object to be lifted when you're taking groceries from the trunk of a car, or a baby from a crib with high sides. At these times it is important to remember to *stabilize* the trunk in the pelvic tilt position so that no twisting or movement of the spine can take place while the spine is being loaded.

You will also notice that when you're lifting objects above your head and your spine begins to arch, it's impossible to hold the pelvic tilt. That's the signal to get a stool or ladder so that the lifting can be accomplished while the trunk is in the balanced pelvic position and potential injury can be averted.

KEEP THE OBJECT CLOSE TO YOUR BODY

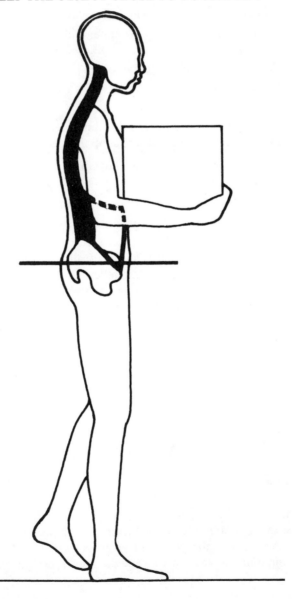

One last word about lifting: keep the object close to your body. There's a rule of physics that explains why this reduces fatigue and strain. The rule states that Work equals Force multiplied by Distance. The further away from the body you hold an object, the more the muscle must work. Try holding a chair with your arms straight out. Now hold it close to your body and you will see how much less effort is required. Take the time to figure out the possibilities—it's worth a few extra minutes for your back's sake.

11

Fitting Your Back to the World You Live In

Every day of our lives we use objects that have, or should have, some relationship to our bodies. Chairs, desks, and furniture can affect our comfort, physical welfare, and performance, according to the way they "fit" us. We are often unaware that the houses we live in, the offices and factories where we work, the cars we drive—even the clothes we wear—have subtle yet significant influences on our bodies. Though it's common knowledge that people aren't as simple as machines, this is often ignored in the artificial environment of the 20th century.

Ergonomics, or as it's called in North America, Human Factors Engineering, is a science devoted to learning how to "fit" the man-made world to people. It's a science made necessary by the Industrial Revolution, which ushered in the factory system and introduced a new element into the lives of workers: the domination of people by machines. For the first time, workers were driven by an inhuman clockwork—their bodies were forced to keep pace with machines powered first by water then by steam. The factory system also introduced cheaper and more efficient methods of producing long standardized runs of goods that were fashioned for the general needs of the masses rather than the specific needs of one person.

It wasn't until World War I, when labour became scarce, that social scientists were stimulated to study the effects of working conditions on human performance, but they were hampered by a lack of knowledge about human anatomy. Very little was accomplished in the study of man and work until World War II gave scientists renewed impetus to study methods of improving the utilization of human resources. In 1949 the Ergonomics Research Society was founded to study the effects of work on man. This scientific body had two main objectives: to enhance the functional effectiveness with which people use their man-made world and to maintain the health, safety, and satisfaction of the workers during the process.

The increased tempo of technological development since World War II has resulted in an epidemic of new and markedly altered types of equipment for human use. If they are designed without appropriate concern for our bodies, there can be unnecessary physical wear and tear as well as accidents. There are three classes of man-made objects we use: (1) man-machine systems, ranging from a man with a hammer up the scale of complexity to an aeroplane or oil refinery; (2) our physical environment, ranging from our homes and workplaces to neighbourhoods or highways; (3) personal items, such as safety shoes and hats, goggles, gloves, all the way up the scale to the astronaut's space-suits.

Ergonomics has become a necessary science. The old trial and error methods of testing had to give way to proper planning if we were to survive the onslaught of the new, highly technical equipment we must deal with in our everyday world.

Static Loading
on Your Back

One of the major problems facing man in the workplace involves a condition called static loading. As we have learned, little modern industrialized work requires isotonic muscular effort. Isometric contractions of the muscles (tension without movement) have become the norm. If the working conditions promote postures requiring inefficient isometric contraction or static loading, a prolonged muscular contraction, which fatigues the muscles, occurs. A long, continuous static work load can lead eventually to an increase in inflammation of the joints and tendon sheaths, and symptoms of arthritis.

Let's look at some examples of static loading on different parts of the body:

1. Bending forward, or stooping for long periods of time will cause static loading of the back muscles.
2. A forward, bent posture of the head—for example, while working at a low table or desk—will cause static loading of the neck muscles.
3. Driving for long periods of time with the arms held straight out will cause static loading of the arm and shoulder muscles.
4. Standing on one leg while working a foot lever on a machine will cause static loading of the leg muscles.

Because we belong to a sit-down generation, where roughly three quarters of us sit down at our work, the predominant effects of static loading take place while we are seated.

At the beginning of this century, the idea gradually emerged that well-being and efficiency improved and fatigue was reduced if people could perform their jobs sitting down. Although this seems a perfectly simple idea, it developed slowly because seating had been considered the perogative of the elite for many centuries. It is possible, in fact, that chairs originated as status symbols, signifying that the chief of the tribe had the right to be raised above the heads of his followers. Even today, seating confers status: the executives of a company have thickly upholstered armchairs, very different from the more functional ones assigned to the employees under them.

No matter what your status, the chair you spend much of your working life in can cause low backache if it places stress on the spine. It has also been discovered by Alf Nachemson, a Swedish orthopaedist, that sitting postures exert more pressure on the discs of the spine than standing ones.

POSTURE	DISC PRESSURE
Standing Erect	100
Lying Flat on Back	24
Sitting with Trunk Erect	140
Sitting Bent Forward	190

Do You Know How To Adjust Your Chair?

Ergonomics experts advise that the best conditions for a relaxed sitting posture involve the following rules: the chair back should be angled five to ten degrees back from the vertical; the seat height should allow the legs to rest on the floor so that the knees are slightly higher than the hips. If you can place your hand between the chair seat and the back of your leg, the height and depth of the seat are correct. If you can't, the chair edge will exert pressure on the thigh and impair proper circulation.

If your working chair doesn't fulfil these qualifications even after you have tried to adjust it, ask your boss to get you a proper chair. Remember that you spend a lot of hours in your chair and it's *your* back that's going to suffer. Many people with back problems hunt persistently for the "perfect chair" but there is no such thing. Because no one position should be maintained indefinitely, the chair that permits the largest number of positions is the best kind for your back.

Making Your Workplace More Comfortable

Here are some ways to make your back more comfortable while you work. A few minor adjustments to the equipment you use can reduce static loading and make a world of difference to your working day.

The office worker

The hazards for office workers involve static loading of the neck, shoulders, and arms because of poor sitting postures and long periods of time spent in one position. You should check out your working equipment with an eye to reducing unnatural stress and loading of the spine. Although I am going to tell you what is best, there will be times when you have to make a tradeoff.

The chair
Have you adjusted it properly for your individual needs? Is it the correct height for you? Is the seat the proper depth and does it support your thighs so that they are slightly above the level of your hips? Does it support your lower back? Is it on castors for easy movement?

The desk
Can you get close to your work? Do the arms of your chair fit under the work surface? Is your desk the proper height? (If it's too low you bend your back, shoulders, and neck and cause static loading; if it's too high, your back will arch and your facet joints will be jammed.) Because most work surfaces are not adjustable you will probably have to adjust your chair up or down to get the correct height. Is there a footrest under the desk? If not, use a large book or small stool to rest your feet on. (This will automatically place the spine in a relaxed position.)

Typing
Make sure your typewriter is on a stand low enough to prevent you from holding your arms too high so that static loading occurs.

Video screen

Position it so that your head does not have to be held at an uncomfortable angle for viewing and you do not suffer from eye strain. Make sure you can hold your arms at a comfortable level while working the keyboard.

Telephone

Use a telephone holder if you must make notes while on the phone. Avoid holding it under your chin. This method of using the phone causes stress in the neck and shoulder muscles.

Exercises for
the office worker

Change your working position whenever possible. Try to fit in different types of work so that your body will have a chance to move. Because women generally need back strengthening, the sit-up and lateral leg lift exercises in the Basic Back Maintenance program are particularly valuable. To relax tight shoulder muscles while in the office perform the arm circles and lateral stretch exercises included in the same program. Try them before your coffee break.

The driver

Statistics show that the longer the time spent driving, the greater the risk of back trouble. Truck drivers and bus drivers are prime candidates for backache because of postural stress from the many hours behind the wheel. We know from Nachemson's studies that sitting increases pressure on the spine. It is, therefore, important for drivers to make sure that their car or truck seats are adjusted properly to eliminate static loading on the spine.

The vehicle

A lot of people drive like cowboys—seat high and as far back as possible, arms and legs held out straight. This posture invites static loading on the arms and legs and stress on the spine. Here are some tips to avoid back fatigue:

1. Make sure your knees are bent and higher than your hips. It could mean that your seat should be moved closer to the wheel than you are used to.
2. The seat should be tilted slightly back and moved closer to the wheel so that your arms can bend at the elbow. If you have arm rests, they can be used to help prevent static loading. The tilted seat allows the back to be more fully supported and gives a better view of the dashboard.

3. Use a contoured backrest if the vehicle seats are too soft. Soft seats discourage movement. Shifting weight and changing positions from time to time help ease the back strain.
4. Because vibration takes a toll of the back, make sure the vehicle's steering, wheel alignment and balance, tires, springs, and shock absorbers are in good condition.
5. Get out of the vehicle and stretch whenever you get the chance. It eases the tension caused by traffic, bad weather conditions, and static loading.

Exercises for
the driver

Sitting at the wheel for hours every day tends to make the abdominal muscles flabby and shortens the psoas muscles. The sit-ups and lateral leg lifts in the Basic Maintenance Exercise program will strengthen and tone the weak abdominal muscles. Particular attention should be paid to the racer's stretch, which will help lengthen the psoas muscles.

To relax and stretch muscles that have become fatigued from tension, arm circles and lateral stretch and calf stretch exercises can be performed while taking a break outside the vehicle.

The executive

A great many executives are hard-driving personalities who, in a sense, get "high" on stress and would feel deprived if they were forced to live more tranquil lives. Postural stress, which causes fatigue in the neck, shoulders, and back muscles and often results in backache can rob the high-powered businessman of the very qualities he prizes most—energy and vitality.

Most executives are well aware of the value of exercise in reducing stress but they go at it the same way they go at life—full out. Because they enjoy testing themselves with power-strength exercises they tend to shy away from the stretch-relaxation types. If poor posture is causing tight, tensed muscles, the stretch-relaxation exercises are needed to loosen up the muscles and prevent back fatigue.

Office
environment

Check the tips on the proper use of furniture under the heading *The Office Worker* to reduce unnecessary static loading and fatigue.

Exercises for
the executive

The stressed executive should perform all of the exercises in the Basic Back Maintenance Exercise program each day. Particular attention should be paid to the breathing techniques that help reduce tension while exercising.

The housewife

As any housewife will tell you, she is emphatically *not* part of the sit-down generation. In fact, she's on her feet for most of a very long day. Because she's physically active and has a lot of variation in her work, ranging from fairly heavy to light duties, the housewife tends to have good flexibility in her back muscles. However, because of the hard work and long hours she puts in, the housewife often needs power exercises to strengthen her back muscles so she will suffer less from fatigue.

When the housewife does have a back problem it has often been initiated by pregnancy. The increased effort put in by the back muscles to counteract the strain of the heavy forward load of the baby can cause backache. This type of backache usually disappears after the baby's birth, but unless exercises are performed to strengthen the back muscles that were stretched during pregnancy, a woman can be left with a weak back, which will worsen with each pregnancy.

There are many ways that the housewife can avoid static loading of her spine. Here's a checklist.

Meal preparation

While you're working at the kitchen counter, rest your back by putting one foot on a small stool. This places your spine in the pelvic tilt position and relaxes it.

Laundry

Read the chapter on lifting techniques. A housewife spends a great deal of time lifting and carrying and the right techniques can save a lot of wear and tear on her spine and prevent back fatigue and injury.

Ironing

Resting one foot on a small stool can prevent back fatigue while standing at the ironing board. Try to vary the activity by sitting down for some types of ironing.

Cleaning

Try to avoid unnecessary bending by using household tools that are designed to prevent static loading on the spine—long-handled feather dusters, upright vacuum cleaners instead of the cannister type, long-handled squeegee mops. While sweeping and vacuuming stand straight and take short strokes to avoid unnecessary bending. Kneel down instead of bending to clean tubs or pick up toys.

Gardening

Kneel down and work at ground level instead of bending. Try to stand straighter while raking and mowing.

Shopping

Apply the principles of good lifting while carrying groceries. Tuck the abdomen into the pelvic tilt position and use it as a hydraulic sac.

Child care

Make sure the equipment for baby tending is adjusted to the proper working height for your needs. Buy a crib with sides that can be easily lowered so you don't have to lean over to lift the child out. Look for lightness and manoeuvrability when buying strollers and the like. Baby carriers that hold the baby in front of the mother, leaving her arms free, are marvellous for both baby and mother. A rocking chair is also a good investment; it exercises the mother's muscles while she is nursing.

Pregnancy

Because it places extra stress on the spine, try not to gain too much weight during pregnancy. On your doctor's advice, perform exercises to promote fitness and easy labour. In the last stages of pregnancy, delegate heavy duties to your husband.

Postnatal

It is unfortunate that postnatal exercises tend to be neglected by new mothers, because they help to counter fatigue and mental depression. Reconditioning exercises will also strengthen back and stomach muscles that were stretched during pregnancy and prevent possible back problems in later years. Pelvic floor conditioning exercises will also prevent future problems and are very simple to perform. Just tighten the buttocks and internal pelvic muscles (as if you were trying to hold back urination), hold for a few seconds, and then relax.

Exercises for
the housewife

If performed each day, the Basic Maintenance Exercise program will keep you in shape. Pay particular attention to the sit-ups and lateral leg lifts, which strengthen the abdominal muscles.

The Athlete

North Americans, for too long just spectators, have now taken to active sports with a passion. Increasing affluence, more leisure time, and a growing awareness that exercise is a "must" for anyone who wants to stay fit have created a nation of sports enthusiasts who jog, run, swim, cycle, and play tennis, squash, and touch football.

Most people are more knowledgeable about the rules of sport than they are about their bodies. They don't realize that not all sports result in stamina, strength, and suppleness, the three requisites of true fitness. In fact, certain sports have an unbalanced effect on the body, an effect which must be remedied by proper supplementary exercise.

Although athletes should be able to score a grade of excellent on the National Back Fitness Test, they may still need special exercises because they are pushing their bodies past the levels of everyday working fitness.

The following tests will determine whether an athlete has optimal flexibility in the key muscles groups. They will also show whether the sport he or she plays has created a muscle imbalance that should be corrected by compensating exercise.

Hamstring Length

This test determines the length of the hamstring muscles at the back of your thigh; they can be shortened and thus weakened by jogging, running, and walking.

Position

Sit on the floor with your arms behind you and your hands on the floor supporting your body. Hold your legs together straight out in front.

Procedure

1. To check the left hamstring, bend your right knee and place your right foot against the inside of your left knee.
2. Extend both arms straight out, parallel to your left leg.
3. Allow your head and trunk to fall forward over your left leg until stopped by pressure in the back of your left thigh.
4. Change legs and repeat procedure to check your right hamstring.

Results

Most children and adults with good flexibility can bend the head forward so that it almost touches the knee. You should be able to bend your head to within three inches of the knee if the hamstring muscles are not tight and shortened.

The Hamstring Stretch in the Back Maintenance Program.

Groin
Length

This test determines the length of your groin muscles, which are located on the inside of your thigh.

Position

Sit on the floor, with your arms behind you and your hands on the floor.

Procedure

1. Bend both legs at the knees and put your feet together, with the soles touching.
2. Position your feet as close as possible to your buttocks and allow your knees to fall outward.

Results

When adults with good flexibility and children perform this test, their knees fall almost down to the floor. Many joggers and adults with stiff, tight muscles will find that their knees remain in an almost vertical position because the groin muscles have been shortened. When one knee remains higher than the other, it usually indicates an old injury or pull to that groin muscle.

Remedy

The Groin Stretch in the Back Maintenance Program.

Calf Length

This one tests the length of your calf muscle, which can be shortened in joggers, runners, and people who constantly wear high heels.

Position

Sit on the floor, with your legs together straight out in front, and your arms behind you supporting your body.

Procedure

Place both feet up against a wall and bend your feet back toward your body.

Results

You should be able to bend your feet back from the vertical to a 30 degree to 40 degree angle. Many people find that almost no movement is possible, especially if there has been an injury to the ankle at one time.

Remedy

The Calf Stretch in the Back Maintenance Program.

Quadriceps
Length

This one determines the length of the quadriceps muscles at the front of your thigh.

Position

Lie face down on the floor with your legs straight out and your arms at your side.

Procedure

1. Bend your right knee, and grasp your right ankle.
2. Bend leg back so that it touches your buttocks.
3. Change legs and repeat.

Result

You should be able to touch your leg to your buttocks with no pain or discomfort in the front of the thigh.

Remedy

The test itself can be performed as an exercise to stretch the quadriceps muscles.

Although excellent for developing cardiovascular stamina and a useful adjunct for weight control because it burns up to 1,000 calories per hour, jogging can be a bad sport if you have a weak back. A compressive jolt (which is delivered from your foot to your knee, up to your hip and your back) is absorbed by the muscles. If jogging is your favourite way to keep fit, strengthen your back by doing the exercises in this book. You should also pay particular attention to the tests for the hamstring and calf muscles, the key ones used in jogging; they can shorten if compensating exercises are not performed.

If you cross country ski or play soccer you should also test your hamstring and calf muscles. Bicycle riders should test their hamstrings and quadriceps for tightness and shortening. Hockey players should test their groin and hamstring muscles. Swimmers don't need to worry—this sport is one of the few totally balanced activities; it develops stamina, strength, and flexibility and is especially good for elderly or handicapped people because there are no gravitational forces for the body to fight.

12

You Wanted to Know: A Backlog of Essential Questions and Answers

QUESTION #1: Does exercise cure back pain?

ANSWER: Emphatically no. Exercise is the last thing anyone should be doing if he or she has back pain. Until the back heals, rest is the appropriate treatment. If you have suffered a back injury, you most certainly will be left with weakened back muscles and this is where exercise comes in. Back exercises strengthen weak back muscles, which can predispose an individual to musculoskeletal strain, the most common cause of low back pain.

QUESTION #2: Am I too old to exercise?

ANSWER: No one's *ever* too old to exercise. The key to life is movement; exercises that loosen stiff, rigid muscles can turn the clock back for anyone, no matter what age. Because aging causes stiffness, exercises that emphasize flexibility rather than strength are the most appropriate for older people, but they should also be cautioned to exercise at a pace and level geared to their special needs.

QUESTION #3: I've been told by my doctor not to do sit-ups. Is it all right for me to try them?

ANSWER: Sit-ups require low back flexibility and strong stomach muscles. Individuals who have had surgery for lumbar fusion and spondylolithesis are often cautioned by doctors not to do them. Because everyone needs strong abdominal muscles to stay in condition, my exercise program offers different types of sit-ups that are geared to protect the individual from injury. The traditional type of sit-up, performed with the feet held or tucked under a couch, is not included in my program. Because people tend to do this type of sit-up rapidly, it can harm a weak back. Instead, I recommend sit-ups that are performed slowly and carefully with the feet on the floor. This method creates a built-in safety factor: if the feet rise off the floor, this immediately signals that a lower level of sit-up—one less arduous and more appropriate to the individual's fitness level—is necessary. If you've been told not to do sit-ups, ask your doctor if the lower level sit-ups included in my exercise program would be suitable for you.

QUESTION #4: Can exercise be effective for a post-surgical patient?

ANSWER: In my opinion, graded exercises done under the direction of a surgeon should be an integral part of post-surgical back care. Surgery to correct certain back problems can have undesirable after-effects, such as muscle atrophy, stiffness, and weaknesses. These can be diminished by a careful exercise regime, which can also help maintain the initial results of corrective surgery. If the back is reconditioned, the need for a possible second or third operation might be averted. When you consider the poor prognosis for these operations you will readily understand why I recommend a corrective exercise program. For example, a recent analysis by the Workman's Compensation Board of Ontario showed the following results after a second back operation: 20% showed some improvement; 60% showed no improvement; 20% suffered from greater pain and disability. Another study of 1015 chronic back sufferers conducted by John McKay, Director of the Industrial Injury Clinic in Neenah, Wisconsin, disclosed that no patient in this study who had had three or more back operations ever returned to work.

QUESTION #5: Is an exercise program beneficial for ankylosing spondylitis?

ANSWER: Ankylosing spondylitis is a disease characterized by inflammation of the joints in the spine, although it can also affect other joints and parts of the body. The inflammation causes stiffness of the affected joints resulting finally in a solid inflexible spinal column sometimes referred to as a "poker spine." This disease commonly begins in young men during their twenties and thirties and is signalled by morning back stiffness that decreases throughout the day. Although it must be treated with anti-inflammatory medication, an exercise program emphasizing flexibility can diminish the sequelae of illness: stiffness, loss of muscle strength, and curvature of the spine. Because of the stiffness in the spine, exercise can be uncomfortable at first and lead to fear and discouragement. Too much enthusiasm, on the other hand, may cause the patient to proceed too quickly. It is, therefore, wise to exercise under the supervision of a physician or physiotherapist.

QUESTION #6: If rest is good for an aching back, why do I wake up with a stiff back after a night's sleep?

ANSWER: In some cases, a stiff back in the morning can indicate a rheumatic process, such as ankylosing spondylitis. In most cases, however, it occurs because of a sleeping position that does not allow the body to move. The body was made for movement even while sleeping, and a soft mattress that prohibits natural body movements during the night can cause back stiffness. So can alcohol or sleeping pills that knock you out and diminish natural body movements while you sleep. Train yourself to sleep in the positions described earlier in the book. They maintain the spine in the balanced pelvic position and allow the back to rest.

QUESTION #7: Can sexual intercourse make my aching back worse?

ANSWER: You've probably heard the old joke, "Backache is the world's greatest contraceptive." But many patients have told me that sex was the last thing they would give up because of backache. And that's great! There is a basic urge for intimacy in all human beings and unless a backache is very severe or it is being used as an excuse to avoid intimacy, most people find ways to carry on. They don't alter their sexual habits. What they do change are their ways of expressing their needs. Let comfort be your guide and avoid positions in which the back will be arched excessively. Don't try to be a hero like the patient who told me that "in the heat of the moment I hung tough." A loving and concerned partner will willingly experiment with positions that provide enjoyment and simulus.

QUESTION #8: Can a cold in the back cause backache?

ANSWER: Unless there are accompanying complaints such as a cough, vomiting, fever or burning urination, a backache is not likely to be caused by a cold. Because the human mind seeks order and explanation, people want a reason for any physical disorder. If there has been no apparent cause for a backache, it is often attributed to a change in the weather or a cold. There is little scientific basis for such beliefs, and as a physician I usually proceed to check the patient out for muscle weakness and imbalance, the more likely causes of the back problem.

QUESTION #9: Should I wear a back brace?

ANSWER: Most authorities agree that a back brace, when prescribed for chronic backache, can improve overall function and performance, but it is only effective as a short-term measure. Because a back brace eliminates flexibility and movement, a long-term reliance on it increases back stiffness and decreases the strength of the supporting musculature, eventually compounding the problems. I have also discovered that most people do not wear a brace bound tightly enough to achieve the maximum effect; that is, to activate the hydraulic sac mechanism so the lifting forces are distributed properly and stress on the spine is diminished. However, patients complain that tight binding causes impaired breathing and discomfort from perspiration during hot weather. It seems a no-win situation. If, however, a back brace helps in the short term, I recommend a back reconditioning program after the brace has been removed.

QUESTION #10: *Can everyone achieve a grade of excellent on the National Back Fitness Test?*

ANSWER: No. It would be unrealistic, for example, to expect older people with back stiffness to ever be able to hit the top score in the sit-up test. The tests have been designed to measure and compare back function and as a method to gauge individual back fitness. Although there are people who will never be able to restore their backs to perfect health, almost all of them can *improve* their level of back fitness. Not only will they look and feel better, they will find that their backs are less likely to succumb to the stresses and strains of everyday living.

QUESTION #11: *Will losing weight fix my back?*

ANSWER: It's not the whole answer but it's certainly a step in the right direction. Running up your weight can run down your back, especially if there is excessive weight on your stomach. Most people know that being overweight can strain the heart and blood vessels but they forget that extra body weight also places unnecessary strain on the lower spinal joints. It's almost impossible for someone who is carrying around a load of weight on the abdomen to stand correctly and so relieve pressure on the lower spine. The excessive stomach weight also stretches the abdominal muscles, weakening them and causing stress on the other back muscles, which are forced to compensate for their poor performance. If you lose weight you can begin to adopt good posture. That, plus back exercises to strengthen your muscles, is the key to a healthy back.

QUESTION #12: *Is your back exercise program appropriate for children?*

ANSWER: The back tests are inappropriate for young children because muscles do not mature until the teen years. If a small child complains of backache, an uncommon disorder in preadolescent years, he or she should be examined by a doctor. The back exercise program can be applied to fully developed teenagers who show weaknesses revealed by the National Back Fitness Test. Parents can help their children develop strong, healthy backs by emphasizing the principles of good back care and posture.

QUESTION #13: I can't believe the clothes I wear can effect my back. Would you explain this statement?

ANSWER: A lot of young people think the tighter the jeans they wear, the sexier they look. Fair enough, but I wish young adults wore looser jeans at work. Tight pants inhibit movement: they sometimes restrict proper bending of the knees and often encourage poor lifting techniques. High-heeled shoes also cause low back pain because they force the body to shift the balance backwards and place more weight-bearing stresses on the delicate facet joints. Many people with chronic low back pain wear earth shoes, which cause the body to shift forward and take the weight off the facet joints. I know that few people are going to give up high heels or tight jeans completely but they can help their backs out by wearing low shoes and looser clothing at work.

QUESTION #14: I've been told that I will have to live with my back pain. Is there no way out for me?

ANSWER: I wish I could guarantee all my patients a life without back pain but the truth is that I don't always know if the pain will permanently disappear. If a backache is caused by a disease, the pain will, of course, depend upon the course of that disease. Backache caused by a musculoskeletal condition is another matter. In this case backache may be caused by problems in the boney, ligamentous, and disc component or from strain, spasm, or weakness in the muscular component. The first component is *unchangeable* except by major medical intervention such as surgery. The second component is *changeable* through a graded reconditioning program. Although I refuse to promise that all back pain will disappear, I do advise my patients that if they do their part and get the back muscles operating at maximum efficiency, at the very best, the pain will disappear and, at the very least, their backs will function better in spite of discomfort.

QUESTION #15: Isn't it harmful to sit with your legs crossed?

ANSWER: I'll answer this question with a question. Why do so many people cross their legs? Simply because it's more comfortable. Getting one knee higher than the hip rests the back and relieves pressure on it. It's a means of resting the back naturally from time to time throughout the day. There is one exception—people with varicose veins who have been specifically instructed by their doctors not to sit with their legs crossed.

QUESTION #16: *I have to lean forward for long periods at my job and it bothers my back. Have you any suggestions?*

ANSWER: There are a number of ways to ease the strain. Bend the knees slightly. Use one arm to support your upper body weight. Put one foot up on an object, say a low stool; this will move the pelvis into the balanced position. Make use of the hydraulic sac technique and tighten your stomach muscles. Change your position frequently.

Abbreviations

Am. Ind. Hyg. Assoc. J.: American Industrial Hygiene Association Journal.
Amer. J. Epidemiol.: American Journal of Epidemiology.
Appl. Ergonomics: Applied Ergonomics.
Br. Med. J.: British Medical Journal.
Canad. Med. Assoc. J.: Canadian Medical Association Journal.
Canad. Med. Assoc.: Canadian Medical Association Journal.
Clin. Med.: Clinical Medicine.
G.P.: General Practitioner.
J. Am. Geriat. Soc.: Journal American Geriatrics Society.
J. Anat.: Journal of Anatomy.
J. Appl. Physiol.: Journal of Applied Physiology.
J. Biomechanics: Journal of Biomechanics.
J. Bone Joint Surg.: The Journal of Bone Joint and Surgery.
J. Med.: Journal of Medicine.
J. Occup. Med.: Journal of Occupational Medicine.
J. Occup. Med: Journal of Occupational Medicine.
J. Safety Res.: Journal of Safety Research.
JAMA: American Medical Association Journal.
JAVMA: Journal American Veterinary Medical Association.
Journal AOA: Journal American Osteopathic Association.
Nat. Safety News: National Safety News.
New Eng. J. Med.: New England Journal of Medicine.
Orthop. Clin. North Am.: Orthopedic Clinics of North America.
Scand J. Rehab. Med.: Scandinavian Journal of Rehabilitation Medicine.
Scand J. Work environ. & health: Scandinavian Journal of Work Environment and Health.

Bibliography

BOOKS

Brown, Frederic W., editor. *Symposium on the Lumbar Spine*, American Academy of Orthopaedic Surgeons, The C. V. Mosley Company, St. Louis, 1981.

Cailliet, R. *Low Back Pain Syndrome*, F.A. Davis Company, Philadelphia, 1968.

Devlin, David. *You and Your Back*, Richard Clay (The Chaucer Press) Ltd., Suffolk, England, 1975.

Finneson, Bernard E. and Freese, Arthur S. *The New Approach to Low Back Pain*, Berkley Publishing Co., J. B. Lippincott Company, Philadelphia, 1973.

Friedmann, Lawrence W. and Galton, Laurence. *Freedom from Backaches*, Simon and Schuster, New York, 1973.

Grandjean, E. *Fitting the Task to the Man*, Taylor and Francis, Ltd., London, 1969.

Hall, Hamilton. *The Back Doctor*, Macmillan of Canada, Toronto, 1980.

Ishmael, William K. and Shorbe, Howard B. *Care of the Back*, J. B. Lippincott Company, Philadelphia, 1969.

Jones, Donald F. *The Cat Stretches*, Dynacopics, Don Mills, Ontario, 1982.

Kraus, Hans. *Backache*, Simon and Schuster, New York, 1965.

Linde, Shirley. *How to Beat a Bad Back*, Rawson, Wade Publishers Incorporated, New York, 1980.

Livingstone, Churchill. *Outline of Orthopaedics*, Longman Group Ltd., London, 1971.

MacNab, Ian. *Backache*, Williams & Wilkins Co., Baltimore, 1977.

Neimark, Paul. *Care of the Back*, Budlong Press Company, Chicago, 1975.

Root, Leon and Kiernan, Thomas. *Oh, My Aching Back*, David McKay Company Inc., New York, 1973.

Schmorl, G. and Junghanns, H. *The Human Spine in Health and Disease*, Grune and Stratton, New York, 1971.

Winter, Ruth. *So You Have...A Pain in the Neck*, Grosset & Dunlap Publishers, New York, 1974.

Wyke, B. *The Lumbar Spine and Back Pain*, Sector Publishing Co., London, 1976.

JOURNAL ARTICLES

Ad Hoc Committee on Low Back X-Rays. "Low back X-rays: criteria for their use in placement examinations in Industry." *J. Occup. Med.* 6:373-380, 1964.

Alston, W., Carolson, K.E., Feldman, D.J., Grimm, Z. and Gerontinos, E. "A Quantitative study of muscle factors in the chronic low back syndrome." *J. Am. Geriat. Soc.* 14:1041-1047, 1966.

Asmussen, E. and Heeboll-Nielsen, K. "Isometric muscle strength of adult men and women." *Communications from Testing and Observation Institute of the Danish National Association for Infantile Paralysis* 11:1-44, 1961.

Ball, M.V., McGuire, J.A., Swaim, J.A. and Hoerlein, B.F. "Patterns of occurence of disk disease among registered dachshunds." *JAVMA*, Volume 180, Number 5, 1982.

Barker, M.E. "Pain in the back and leg: a general practice survey." *Rheumatology and Rehabilitation* 16:37-45, 1977.

Bartelink, D.L. "The role of abdominal pressure in relieving the pressure on the lumbar intervertebral discs." *J. Bone Joint Surg.* 39B:718-725, 1957.

Beals, R.K. and Hickman, N.W. "Industrial injuries of the back and extremities." *J. Bone Joint Surg.* 54-A:1593-1611, 1972.

Beasley, W.C. "Quantitative muscle testing: principles and applications to research and clinical services." *Archives of Physical Medicine & Rehabilitation* 42:398-425, 1961.

Becker, W.F. "Prevention of low back disability." *J. Occup. Med.* 3:329-335, 1961.

Benn, R.T. and Wood, P.H.N. "Pain in the back: an attempt to estimate the size of the problem." *Rheumatology and Rehabilitation* 14:121-128, 1975.

Berkson, M., Schultz, A., Nachemson, A. and Andersson, G. "Voluntary strengths of male adults with acute low back syndromes." *Clinical Orthopaedics and Related Research* no. 129, 84-95, 1977.

Bernauer, E.M. and Bonanno, J. "Development of physical profiles for specific jobs," *J. Occup. Med.* 17:27-33, 1975.

Brown, J.R. "Lifting as an industrial hazard." *Am. Ind. Hyg. Assoc. J.* 34:292-297, 1973.

Cady, L.D., Bischoff, D.P., O'Connell, E.R., Thomas, P.C. and Allan, J.H. "Strength and fitness and subsequent back injuries in firefighters." *J. Occup. Med.* 21:269-272, 1979.

Caldwell, L.S., Chaffin, D.B., Dukes-Dobos, F.N., Kroemer, K.H.E., Laubach, L.L., Snook, S.H. and Wasserman, D.E. "A proposed standard procedure for static muscle strength Testing." *Am. Ind. Hyg. Assoc. J.* 35:201-205, 1974.

Chaffin, D.B. "Human strength capability and low back pain." *J. Occup. Med.* 16:248-254, 1974.

Chaffin, D.B. and Park, K.S. "A longitudinal study of low-back pain as associated with occupational weight lifting factors." *Am. Ind. Hyg. Assoc. J.* 34:12, 513-525, 1973.

Chaffin, D.B. "Ergonomics guide for the assessment of human static strength." *Am. Ind. Hyg. Assoc. J.* 36:505-510, 1975.

Chaffin, D.B. and Moulis, E.J. "An empirical investigation of low back strains and vertebrae geometry." *J. Biomech.* 2:89-97, 1970.

Chaffin, D.B.; Herrin, G.D. and Keyserling, W.M. "Pre-employment strength testing - an updated position." *J. Occup. Med.* 20:403-408, 1978.

Clark, A.B. and Russek, A.S. "Back injuries." In: *Rehabilitation in Industry*, D.A. Covalt, Ed. Grune and Stratton, New York, 1958.

Corlett, E.N. and Bishop, R.P. "A technique for assessing postural discomfort." *Ergonomics* . 19:175-182, 1976.

Cumming, G.R. "Current levels of fitness." *Canad. Med. Assoc. J.* 96:868-882, 1967.

Currey, H.L.F., Greenwood, R.M., Lloyd, G.G. and Murray, R.S. "A prospective study of low back pain." *Rheumatology and Rehabilitation* 18:94-104, 1979.

Davis, P.R. "Posture of the trunk during the lifting of weights." *Br. Med. J.* 1:87-89, 1959.

Dehlin, O., Hedenrud, B. and Horal, J. "Back symptoms in nursing aides in a geriatric hospital." *Scand J. Rehab. Med.* 8:47-53, 1976.

Dively, R.L. and Oglevie, R.R. "Pre-employment examinations of the low back." *JAMA* 60:85-86, 1956

Farfan, H.F. "The effects of torsion on the lumbar intervertebral joints: The role of torsion in the production of disc degeneration." *J. Bone Joint Surg.* 52A:468-483, 1970.

Farfan, H.F. "A reorientation in the surgical approach to degenerative lumbar intervertebral joint disease." *Orthopaedic Clinics of North Am.* 8,1,9-21, 1977.

Frymoyer, J.W., Pope, M.H., Costanza, M.C., Rosen, J.C., Goggin, J.E. and Wilder, D.G. "Epidemiologic studies of low back pain." *Spine* 5:419-422, 1980.

Gerard, W. "The dream of a painless body." *Maclean's* December, 60-72, 1980.

Gibson, E.S., Martin, R.H. and Terry, C.W. "Incidence of low back pain and pre-placement X ray screening." *J. Occup. Med.* 22:515-519, 1980.

Gimlett, D.M. "The back X ray controversy." *J. Occup. Med.* 14:785-786, 1972.

Gunn, C.C., Milbrandt, W.E. and Little, A. "Peripheral nerve injuries mimicking lumbar disc herniations." *BC Medical Journal* 19:350-352, 1977.

Gunn, C.C. and Milbrandt, W.E. "The neurological mechanism of needle-grasp in acupuncture." *American Journal of Acupuncture* 5:115-120, 1977.

Gunn, C.C. "Tenderness at motor points." *J. Bone Joint Surg.* 58A:815-825, 1976.

Gunn, C.C. "Utilizing trigger points." *The Osteopathic Physician* March, 29-52, 1977.

Gunn, C.C. "Tenderness at motor points: an aid in the diagnosis of pain in the shoulder referred from the cervical spine." *Journal AOA* 77:196-212, 1977.

Gunn, C.C. "'Bursitis' around the hip." *American Journal of Acupuncture* 5:53-60, 1977.

Gunn, C.C. "Early and subtle signs in low back sprain." *Spine* 3:267-281, 1978.

Gyntelberg, Finn. "One year incidence of low back pain among male residents of Copehagen aged 40-59." *Danish Medical Bulletin* 21:30-36, 1974.

Hanman, B. "The evaluation of physical ability." *New. Eng. J. Med.* 258:986-993, 1958.

Harley, W.J. "Lost time back injuries: Their relationship to heavy work and preplacement back X-rays." *J. Occup. Med.* 14:511-614, 1972.

Herrin, G.D. and Chaffin, D.B. "Effectiveness of strength testing." *Professional Safety*, Park Ridge, USA, Vol. 23, No. 7, 39-43, 51.

Hirsch, T. "The billion dollar backache." *Nat. Safety News.* May, 1977.

Hrubec, Z., and Nashold, B.S. "Epidemiology of lumbar disc lesions in the military in World War II." *Amer. J. Epidemiol.* 102:367-376, 1975.

Jones, D.F. "From baseball to the moon." *Canadian Occup. Safety Magazine*, Part I, Nov. 1969, 7:6, Part II, Jan. 1970, 8:1.

Jones, D.F. "Back strains: The state of the art." *J. Safety Res.* 3:38-41, 1971.

Kamon, E. and Goldfuss, A.J. "In-plant evaluation of the muscle strength of workers." *Am. Ind. Hyg. Assoc. J.* 39:801-807, 1978.

Kelly, F.J. "Evaluating musculoskeletal capabilities - A practical approach." *J. Occup. Med.* 17:266-269, 1975.

Keyserling, W.M., Herrin, G.D. and Chaffin, D.B. "Isometric strength testing as a means of controlling medical incidents on strenuous jobs." *J. Occup. Med.* 22:332-336, 1980.

Kosiak, M., Aurelius, J.R. and Harfield, W.F. "Backache in industry." *J. Occup. Med.* 8:51-58, 1966.

Kraus, H. "Prevention of low back pain." *J. Occup. Med.* 9:555-559, 1967.

Kraus, H. "Diagnosis and treatment of low back pain." *G.P.* 5:55 1952.

Kraus, H. and Hirschland, R.P. "Muscular fitness and orthopedic disability." *New York J. Med.* 54:212 1954.

Kraus, H., Melleby, A. and Gaston, S.R. "Back pain correction and prevention." *New York State Journal of Med.* 77:1335-1338, 1977.

LaRocca, H. and MacNab, I. "Value of pre-employment radiographic assessment of the lumbar spine." *Canad. Med. Assoc. J.* 101:383-388, 1969.

Levy, L.F. "Lumbar intervertebral disc disease in Africans." *Journal of Neurosurgery* 26:31-34, 1967.

Magora, Alexander. "Investigation of the relation between low back pain and occupation." *Scand. Rehab. Med.* 7:146-151, 1975.

Magora, A. "Investigation of the relation between low back pain and occupation." *Ind. Med.* 41:5-9, 1972.

Mantle, M.J., Greenwood, R.M. and Currey, H.L.F. "Backache in pregnancy." *Rheumatology and Rehabilitation* 16:95-101, 1977.

Mayer, Leo and Greenberg, B.B. "Measurements of the strength of trunk muscles." *J. Bone Joint Surg.* 24:842-856, 1942.

McGill, C.M. "Industrial back problems: A control program." IT J. Occup. Med. 10:174-176, 1968.

McKenzie, R.A. "Manual correction of sciatic scoliosis." *New Zealand Medical Journal* 76:194-199, 1972.

Montgomery, C.H. "Pre-employment back X-rays." *J. Occup. Med.* 18:495-498, 1976.

Morris, J.M., Lucas, D.B. and Bresler, B. "Role of the trunk in stability of the spine." *J. Bone Joint Surg.* 43A:327-351, 1961.

Nachemson, A. "Low back pain, its etiology and treatment." *Clin. Med.* 78:18-24, 1971.

Nummi, J., Jarvinen, T., Stambej, U. and Wickström, G. "Diminished dynamic performance capacity of back and abdominal muscles in concrete reinforcement workers." *Scand. J. Work Environ. & Health* 4:39-46, 1978.

Ohara, H., Nakagiri, S., Itani, T., Wake, K. and Aoyama, H. "Occupational health hazards resulting from elevated work rate situations." *Journal of Human Ergology* 5:173-182, 1976.

Onishi, N. and Nomura, H. "Low back pain in relation to physical work capacity and local tenderness." *Journal of Human Ergology* 2:119-132, 1973.

Pace, J.B. "Commonly overlooked pain syndromes responsive to simple therapy." *Postgraduate Medicine* 58:107-113, 1975.

Pace, J.B. and Nagle, D. "Piriform syndrome." *The Western Journal of Medicine* 124:435-439, 1976.

Pannier, S. and Nahon, E. "Prévention et traitement en milieu de travail hospitalier des lombalgies professionnelles par une rééducation visée prophylactique." (Prevention and treatment of occupational low back pain in hospital workers by prophylactic muscular rehabilitation.) *Archives des maladies professionnelles* 39:469-482, 1978.

Pederson, O.F., Petersen, R. and Staffeldt, E.S. "Back pain and isometric back muscle strength of workers in a Danish factory." *Scand. J. Rehab. Med.* 7:125-128, 1975.

Pheasant, H.C. "Backache - its nature, incidence and cost." *The Western Journal of Medicine* 126:330-332, 1977.

Poulson, E. and Jorgenson, K. "Back muscle strength, lifting and stoop working postures." *Appl. Ergonomics* 1:133-137, 1971.

Ratcliffe, J.D. "I am Joe's spine." *The Reader's Digest* Reprint, March, 1971.

Redfield, J.T. "The low back X-ray as a pre-employment screening tool in the forest products industry." *J. Occup. Med.* 13:219-226, 1971.

Rowe, M.L. "Low back pain in industry: A position paper." *J. Occup. Med.* 11, 1969.

Rowe, M.L. "Low back disability in industry: Updated position." *J. Occup. Med.* 13:10, 476-478, 1971.

Runge, Carl F. 'Rocntgrnographic examinations of the lumbarocal in routine pre-employment examination." *J. Bone & Joint Surg. 36-A:75, 1954.*

Snook, S.H. "The design of manual handling tasks." *Ergonomics .* 21:963-985, 1978.

Snook, S.H. and Ciriello, V.M. "Maximum weights and work loads acceptable to female workers." *J. Occup. Med.* 16:527-534, 1974.

Snook, S.H. and Irvine, C.H. "Maximum acceptable weight of lift." *Am. Ind. Hyg. Assoc. J.* 28:322-329, 1967.

Snook, S.H.; Irvine, C.H. and Bass, S.F. "Maximum weights and workloads acceptable to male industrial workers." *Am. Ind. Hyg. Assoc. J.* 31:579-586, 1970.

Snook, S.H. "Maximum frequency of lift acceptable to male industrial workers." *Am. Ind. Hyg. Assoc. J.*, Vol. 29, Nov.-Dec. 1968; reprinted in *American Society of Safety Engineers Journal*, August 1969.

Tichauer, E.R. "Some aspects of stress on forearm and hand in industry." *J. Occup. Med.* 8:63-71, 1966.

Tichauer, E.R.; Miller, G. and Nathan, I. "Lordosimetry: A new technique for the measurement of postural response to materials handling." *Am. Ind. Hyg. Assoc. J.* 34:1-12, 1973.

Troup, J.D.G. and Chapman, A.E. "The static strength of the lumbar erectores spinae." *J. Anat.* 105:186, 1968.

Troup, J.D.G. and Chapman, A.E. "The strength of the flexor and extensor muscles of the trunk." *J. Biomechanics* 2:49-62, 1969.

Troup, J.D.G. "Relation of lumbar spine disorders to heavy manual work and lifting." *The Lancet*, April 17, 1965.

White, A.W.M. "Low back pain in men receiving workmen's compensation." *Can. Med. Assoc. J.* 95:50-56, 1966.

Whitney, R.J. "The strength of the lifting action in man." *Ergonomics .* 1:101-128, 1958.

Woodson, W. "Good human engineering is possible using off the shelf component products." *Human Factors* 13:141-152, 171.

ADDITIONAL ARTICLES

Ayoub, M.M. and McDaniel, J.W. "Predicting Lifting Capacity." Paper presented at the Fifth Congress on Ergonomics, Amsterdam, Holland, 1973.

Ayoub, M.M., Dryden, R.D. and Knipfer, R.E. "Psychophysical Based Models for the Prediction of Lifting Capacity of the Industrial Worker." Paper presented at the Automotive Engineering Congress and Exposition (SAE), Detroit, 1976.

Brown, J.R. *Lifting as an Industrial Hazard.* Labour Safety Council of Ontario, Ontario Dept. Labor, Ontario, Canada, 1971.

Chaffin, D.B. "Manual Materials Handling and Low Back Pain." In: *Occupational Medicine, Principles and Practical Applications.* C. Zenz, Ed. Year Book Medical Publishers, Inc., Chicago, 1975.

Davis, P.R. and Troup, J.D.G. "Effects on the Trunk of Handling Loads in Different Postures." Proc. Second Internat. Cong. Ergonomics, Dortmund, 1964.

Hoerlin, B.F. "Comparative Disk Disease: Man and Dog." School of Veterinary Medicine, Auburn, Alabama, Number 1343, 1978. Industrial Accident Prevention Association. Update Release on Back Injuries, 1979. International Labour Organization. "Manual Lifting and Carrying." *Int. Occup. Safety Health Inform.* Sheet ç3, Geneva, 1962. International Labour Organization. "Maximum Permissible Weight to Be Carried by One Worker." ILO Office, Geneva, 1964-1967. International Labour Office. "Encyclopaedia of occupational health and safety." 2 vols., 1972.

Mumford, Ted. "Backing Up Our Backs." *Workmans Compensation Board Report,* 1980.

Munchinger, R. "Manual Lifting." International Labour Organization, Geneva, 1962.

Robertson, C.M. "A Review of Back Injury Claims at the British Columbia Workers' Compensation Board," 1977.

Scneider, M. Franz. "An Investigation into the Effect of Concrete Reinforcement Work on Degenerative Back Disease and Back Injury." Ontario Ministry of Labour, 1979.

Index